TAMING CHAOS

HARNESSING THE POWER OF KABBALAH
TO MAKE SENSE OF OUR LIVES

KABBALIST RAV P.S. BERG

For further information contact:
The Kabbalah Centre™
Director Rav Berg
1-800-KABBALAH™   www.kabbalah.com™
1062 S. Robertson Blvd, Los Angeles, CA 90035
155 E. 48th Street, New York, NY 10017

First Edition, Released as "Secret Codes of the Universe", April 2000
Second Edition June 2003. Printed in USA

ISBN 1-57189-225-7

לבריאות, הצלחה, אהבה ואחדות

למשה בן חיים אברהם

רות בת אברהם

רינה בת אהרון

וכל משפחותיהם

יעקב בן חיים

פרננדה בת אברהם

ולכל הילדים

CONTENTS

For my wife

Karen

In the vastness of cosmic space and

the infinity of lifetimes, it is my

bliss to share a soul mate and an age

of Aquarius with you.

INTRODUCTION:

THE PROMISE OF KABBALAH

Whatever was is that which shall be, and that which was done is what shall be done, for there is nothing new under the sun.

—Proverbs 1:9

The Trees of Life and Knowledge

Germany produces Nietzsche and Beethoven, then deifies Adolf Hitler and follows him into war. The United States—beacon of hope and citadel of freedom for the world—struggles with a history of slavery and prejudice. Some young people strive for academic excellence or reach for Olympic gold while others drop out of school to wear stolen gold and roam inner city streets as a new breed of ruthless super-predator.

Dr. Jekyll, meet Mr. Hyde—right there in the mirror. Humankind is at once the glory and the shame of the universe. The glory is built-in; He who created us does not make mistakes. We, alone, are responsible for the shame. Every self-serving, negative act we commit contributes to the darkness that threatens to engulf the universe. And those acts of negativity, from the most heinous of crimes to the pettiest of "sins," eventually rebound upon every one of us in a legacy of disease, disaster, depression, and death. It is a monotonous cycle that vindicates the old cliché, "what goes around, comes around," and presents life as little more than a carousel in a nightmare.

1

But it doesn't have to be that way. We can seize control of our lives, banish evil, and fill our souls with Light simply by applying the principles of what can now be legitimately called the science of Kabbalah.

According to the new science of quantum physics, all matter is reduced at the subatomic level to six quarks, three forces, and three leptons. According to the ancient metaphysics of Kabbalah, the cosmos is reduced at the metaphysical level to simply two energy systems: the Tree of Life and the Tree of Knowledge. It will be seen in the course of this treatise that the new physics and the old metaphysics are completely complementary. In fact, science of the late 20th century has made it possible for Kabbalah to be taught to the world at large and not to just a few scholars. Science has provided the world with a comprehensible frame of reference to access Kabbalah.

Most of us sense that we are not an isolated entity in the universe; we are an integral part of all that exists—an extension of something as infinitesimal as an atom, and as infinite as the energy that fuels the stars and drives the galaxies. But physical energy systems are not the only ones that affect us. Metaphysical energy systems also affect our lives, for better or for worse, and their study is what this book is all about.

Genesis Revisited

The Book of Genesis gives us one of the most powerful images of the creation of the world: "In the beginning, God created the heaven and the earth. And the earth was without form and void; and darkness was upon the face of the deep. And the Spirit of God moved upon the face of the waters. And God said, 'Let there be Light; and there was Light. And God saw the Light, that it was good.'" (Genesis 1–4).

In the beginning, then, with the Big Bang still reverberating through a newborn universe, the Light was all that was good. In all of Creation, there was nothing of consciousness, save the Creator, and despite omniscience and omnipotence on a scale beyond mortal comprehension, the Creator was lonely. The Creator, after all, was and is the Light—a powerful outpouring of purity and beneficence. In the beginning there were no vessels to hold the endless bounty of His beneficence, and so, with nothing more than desire, He created those vessels, our souls, as the living desire to receive from His exalted Light.

Creation was thus infused with an inherent contradiction. Not even He could create without imbuing the Creation with His own essence, and His only essence is a desire to share. Therefore, our souls instantly were conflicted between the created desire to receive and the imbued desire to share. And so, we were born with shame, the shame of receiving so much and giving nothing in return.

With shame came our first act of free will, an act that led to the first restriction in a hitherto unrestricted universe: *en masse*, we said "no" to the Creator. If we could not share and prove ourselves worthy of His bounty by paying our own way, we would, in effect, have no more of what He so freely gave. Only if we could earn His gift would it cease to be a gift and thus remove the "Bread of Shame"—the self-destructive emotions that result from receiving unearned beneficence. Only then could we earn the Creator's beneficence by learning to share what we received.

Kabbalah, which means literally "to receive," is shared here now for all to apply, in a world that never needed it more. It proposes a second Genesis: "In the beginning" all over again, with untold bounty for all who have the determination to follow its way.

Nothing New Under the Sun

Electricity was not born when Benjamin Franklin went out in a thunderstorm and launched his famous kite and key—it had been waiting silently in the wings since the world's debut lightning bolt. Nuclear power did not come into being in a laboratory in Los Alamos, nor did it make its debut in the first atomic bomb. It has fueled the stars since the Big Bang. Sir Isaac Newton did not invent gravity and Albert Einstein did not create relativity. They were in existence long before midwives placed the discoverers in the arms of their mothers.

As the proverb says, "There is nothing new under the sun." But there are new uses for ancient powers. We just need to increase our understanding of the universe and our place in it.

How do we harness the power that is within us? No contractor would attempt to wire a house without using a schematic for guidance. To bring the power of electricity into a dwelling without burning it down, you need a system consisting of three lines: a hot wire, a neutral, and a ground. If you mis-wire the circuitry anywhere along the line, you risk a blown fuse—or a three-alarm blaze.

Life is a lot like that. Most of us never really learn how to wire our lives. We rely on the convenience of electricity and if we sometimes stop to consider the dangers of the nuclear reactors and other power plants that produce it, we rarely think about the potentially dangerous power coursing through our homes. And most of us remain in an unlit cave in terms of understanding our spiritual power. As a result, we go through life blowing fuses, starting fires, and causing meltdowns. Generally, we make a chaotic mess of things.

Human beings have always felt the pull of the infinite power and mystery of the universe. How did we get here and why do we exist? The roads traveled toward those questions are many, the answers few and far between. As we grope our way along the dark tunnel to enlightenment, our efforts invariably are impeded or abused by false prophets, false friends, and our own misguided stabs at following the pursuit of happiness.

The 21st century has dawned in a welter of wars and rumors of wars, of "ethnic cleansing," of terrorists both foreign and domestic. Husbands brutalize wives, fathers abuse children, mothers make drug addicts of their fetuses, and kids who are barely teenagers commit mass murder in the schoolyard. As the human race seems to sink lower and lower, one cannot help but wonder if evangelical cries of the end of the world may not be closer to the truth than we would like to think. Whether they are or not, it is incumbent upon men and women everywhere to learn how to take control of their lives and avoid the collision with extinction, a course humankind appears to be headed toward.

Here is the simple truth: we can change everything with a power so mysterious it defies the minds of the greatest scientists, yet so simple that small children use it without thinking. This power is called Kabbalah, and with it we can rewire our lives.

Kabbalah stems directly from the heart and soul of Judaism and therefore employs biblical terms in its vocabulary. But make no mistake: Kabbalah is no more a religion than is quantum mechanics, with which it shares a distinct affinity. Kabbalah is universal. And though it posits the existence of a Creator, it is not designed for worship. Kabbalah is designed for use—the most profound metaphysical use the world has ever known. The rights and privileges that go along with using Kabbalah are now the property of the people. Unlike traditional religion, there is no need for intermediaries—rabbis, priests, or shamans—to help one connect to the forces of Creation. This fact alone explains the clergy's ongoing opposition to public dissemination of Kabbalah.

The energy system employed by Kabbalah is called the Tree of Life, a term that refers to a reality that lies beyond our limited five senses. It is a realm of infinite fulfillment and order. It is the source of our intuition and sixth sense, the place from which pleasure, joy, healing, and happiness originate. And though we may not physically touch and see this reality, it is as undeniable as gravity and as real as the atoms in the air.

The Tree of Life comes equipped with a blueprint designed to tell the humblest of us exactly how to use it. (This will be explained in detail in chapter 1.) Although the secrets of the Tree of Life have been around for eternity, they have only now become accessible; the technological and scientific wonders of the 20th century have made it possible for us to comprehend their mysteries. And this powerful knowledge comes just in time.

Science Is Dead, Long Live Science

This world we now live in is marked by the ascendancy of Albert Einstein and a new cadre of visionary scientists like Stephen Hawking. Einstein's physics and quantum mechanics replaced the Newtonian model; radical concepts such as the uncertainty principle became established and inherent. Then, we began to understand the universe as a place of random chaos in which, at the subatomic level, matter simply ceased to exist.

Suddenly, it was as if the world had lost its grounding. Certainty about the nature of reality ceased to exist and humankind was plunged into a penetrating fear of the unknown, which the early Kabbalistic writers knew to be the most terrifying of all human fears, since what is not known can neither be controlled nor avoided. Our new scientific worldview gives us much new information to absorb about our surroundings. It also places a burden upon us to find a way to restore structure in our daily universe.

If we are to become masters of our destiny, then let us begin by accepting the idea that constitutes the first step toward all Kabbalistic power and methodology: an effort is required on our part. Unfortunately, we have become a society that believes it can purchase instant relief and gratification for most things that ail us. This approach leads us down a road toward disaster. As most people immediately sense, there are no shortcuts to achieving permanence in our well-being. This book offers no instant VIP passport to the portals of Kabbalistic power. The would-be practitioner must be willing to work for it by stretching his or her mind, developing techniques of prayer and meditation, and even learning the Hebrew alphabet, since the letters contained therein are the building blocks of understanding

Kabbalah. One need not be fluent in the language—in many cases it is necessary only to visualize the letters in order to access their power—but one should become at least phonetically proficient, because other uses call for a proper pronunciation of each letter and word. For those who are willing to persevere in the study and practice of Kabbalah, the rewards can be immense.

The next step, simply, is a resolve to develop a positive attitude toward our neighbors and our environment. The cosmos is full of a negative energy created by humans, and most of us have experienced the difficulties of operating against that self-perpet-uating, human-made, negative force field. There are endless techniques, therapies, and self-help books that offer some assis-tance in overcoming the obstacles of negativity. Their help, however, can and will be of only a temporary nature. To affect permanent mastery over our lives and destinies, we must change the nature of our behavior. That requires a new kind of knowl-edge not found in self-help books.

The Unseen Becomes Visible

A few years ago, television sets in England suddenly started picking up the programming of a Texas station. Under normal circumstances, that would not have seemed strange, for Earth's ever-undulating atmosphere is capable of producing all manner of weird anomalies, allowing broadcast signals to skip and hop far beyond their normal range. But this was a far more puzzling event. The Texas station in question had been defunct for decades; the ghostly signal picked up in England had first been broadcast in the 1950s.

Television stations die, but their programming lives on—most of it making its way at light speed out into deep space. Our bodies die, but our immortal souls do not. Why should it be different with our thoughts and actions? Every negative word, every negative act ever uttered or committed, lives on, adversely impacting human lives long after their authors have left the scene. As a result, we are swamped, as never before, living in all the negativity that ever was. Only through Kabbalah can the torrent be reversed to bring order out of chaos and make music out of noise.

Right now, the world is plugged into the wrong energy system. This system is called the Tree of Knowledge—another code phrase. In this phrase, knowledge is a misnomer, an illusion, a lure. Metaphorically, this is the same tree bearing the forbidden fruit that resulted in the eviction of Adam and Eve from the Garden of Eden.

The Tree of Knowledge refers to the physical universe we perceive with our five senses. It refers to the world of chaos, calamity, and confusion. This energy system is founded upon the human desire to receive, but only for the self alone. In the Tree of Knowledge, receiving means greed. It means selfishness and self-indulgence. Those who have invested themselves in this way of living will receive and receive, and yet, in the long run, they will gain nothing because what they receive is devoid of energy—as empty as an electrical circuit that, through being hooked up incorrectly, has blown its fuse.

Turn On the Lights

Unlike the Tree of Knowledge, which arises from imperfect human understanding, the Tree of Life emanates from the Light of the Creator. It, too, is based upon the human desire to receive, though in a higher form—the desire to receive for the sake of sharing. The power of this kind of receiving is immense and, best of all, available to all who would access it. Those hooked into the Tree of Life will give as much as they receive and, as a result, will want for nothing, because what they receive is charged with energy.

This cosmic power source consists of what Kabbalists call Sfirot (Sfira in the singular)—essentially packets of bottled-up energies, each with its own intelligence and individual attributes. The Sfirot are the metaphysical equivalents of what quantum physicists call quanta—the energy sources that construct the cosmos.

The Tree of Life contains ten Sfirot, (which will be described in chapter 1), and can be envisioned as constructed of three columns. The right branch is sometimes known as the male side and can be seen as the positive side, the benevolent side. The left, or negative, branch has a sterner aura, representing power and judgment, and is known as the female side. The central column holds the two branches in delicate balance. The left column is not "better" or more positive in a moral sense than the right. Rather, like the negative and positive ends of an electrical wire, both are necessary to make true light happen. These energies are intricately and ultimately linked. It is in the linking and balance of positive and negative that we find power.

The Zohar

Four actions are required of those who would balance these forces, understand the Tree of Life, and access the freedom it offers. They are restriction, sharing, meditation, and prayer. These are everyday, familiar actions, which are almost innate to human nature, and yet most of us have never been taught the right way to engage in them.

Luckily, there exists an "owner's manual" that has been around for some 2,000 years. It is called the Zohar, or Book of Splendor. It is one of the most important canonical books of Judaism and a complete codification of Kabbalah, the origins of which go back to Abraham, the patriarch.

Kabbalah was wielded in the days of Genesis and Exodus like a mighty sword. Moses drew from its power in order to find a way to part the Red Sea and rescue his people from Pharaoh's army, and again to draw water from a stone in the barren desert of Sinai. Yet thousands of years passed before its principles were set down by a great sage and mystic, Rabbi Shimon bar Yohai. Driven into hiding by a Roman emperor who forbade the teaching of Judaism, and under the threat of death, Rabbi Shimon and his son, Rabbi Eleazar, retreated to a secret cave where, in the course of 13 years, they wrote the Zohar.

The Zohar foresaw that one day humankind would seize control over its destiny by finally learning to grasp the profound mysteries of the cosmos and thereby eliminate the constant turmoil of human society. That time is now. The key to the Tree of Life, and to the meaning of restriction, sharing, meditation, and prayer, is in the Zohar.

The schematic of electrical circuitry is an excellent metaphor for the Tree of Life. The negative left-hand column is analogous to the hot wire that brings the power into the home; the positive right-hand column represents the neutral force, returning the circuit flow. The balancing central column is the filament that glows with light as a result of its resistance, or restriction of energy. By restricting our inborn desire to receive—by saying, "No, I will not take it all; I will leave some for someone else"— we convert that desire into a new and much greater positive energy. Restricting our desires and discovering the desire to share are the first two steps in the journey to becoming much more than we have been.

The Zohar teaches that meditation and prayer are the metaphysical links connecting human beings to the celestial Light. Prayer is designed to stabilize our lives; it is the communication system by which humans fulfill the original purpose of their existence as determined in Genesis, which is one of returning to and dwelling within the energy of the Tree of Life.

Most prayers are recited in a robotic state of consciousness and are used as shortcuts for alleviating sorrow or mending the consciences of evildoers. From the Kabbalistic viewpoint, this kind of prayer is wholly insufficient.

Meditation is the key to proper prayer. Kabbalistic meditation is closely allied with prayer, but distinct from all other techniques. The Zohar says that without a proper meditation for any particular prayer, the words of that prayer will fall short of their mark. A directed-meditation system is an integral element in achieving spiritual growth. When performed properly, prayer is an extremely powerful instrument to help us achieve control over our lives, our environment, and our destinies.

The Cosmic Illusion

The Kabbalistic journey prepares us for entry into the consciousness of the Tree of Life, where chaos and disorder will be recognized for what they are—an illusion. Kabbalah and Kabbalistic meditation teach us the way to remove ourselves from the spiritually impoverishing cycle of negativity, struggle, failure, and ultimate defeat.

A prayer that falls short of connection to the Tree of Life cannot provide quantum control, and anything less than quantum control must, of necessity, drag us down to the Tree of Knowledge with its illusory realm of good and evil. This book will serve as a guide to discovery of the cosmic power sources of the Tree of Life and show that it is possible to acquire immunity from the chaos known as death.

But that is not the only "miracle" taught to us by the Zohar. Once we have acquired the knowledge of parallel universes, which the Tree of Life and the Tree of Knowledge embody, our expanded awareness and consciousness will open us up to the mysteries of what has recently been named the "paranormal."

Without establishment of a quantum prayer consciousness, which includes multiple channels and methods of approach, the reality of the Tree of Life appears to be beyond our immediate perspective. Yet, if we truly desire to attain our inalienable right to acquire happiness and fulfillment in our daily lives, the Tree of Life and its reality become visible.

Taming Chaos

The Kabbalist knows that the fundamental underlying cause of the difficulties and chaotic conditions that have become part of the human landscape is the intolerance of people toward their fellow humans. For this reason, the Holy Temple in Jerusalem was destroyed. The Jews of that dark day caused humankind to be severed from the Light of the Creator, and this permitted negative energy to overtake the world. What happened then was the creation of a phenomenon that has been designated by the Talmud as Sinat Hinam: hatred without reason.

Sinat Hinam represents the desire to receive for the self alone, a state found in the Tree of Knowledge. It manifests itself whenever an individual who lacks nothing in this material world notices that his or her neighbors also lack nothing and hates them for it. If you cannot bear the sight of another person who possesses that which you, too, possess, then you link yourself to an energy system that will, in one way or another, eventually cost you everything, right down to your immortal soul.

This book is designed as a kind of layperson's handbook, a guide to arm the reader against any of the illusory misfortunes or packets of chaotic energy that occur in our daily lives. More important, the Kabbalistic meditation techniques presented here will create security shields to help dematerialize the pain and suffering that seems to be the trademark of humankind, thus reversing the trend of predictable disorder and unhappiness.

CHAPTER 1

THE TREE OF LIFE AND THE TREE OF KNOWLEDGE

What a Chimera then is man! What a novelty! What a monster, what a chaos, what a contradiction, what a prodigy! Judge of all things, feeble earthworm, depository of truth, a sink of uncertainty and error, the glory and the shame of the universe.

—Blaise Pascal, 1623–1662

A Startling Discovery

The average citizen made no note of it. There were no headlines in the daily newspapers and the occasion was marked by no sound bytes on television, but in July 1992, two scientists from the Massachusetts Institute of Technology stood the universe on its head. Astronomer Jack Wisdom and computer scientist Gerald Sussman published an article in the journal Science in which they announced that, contrary to conventional wisdom, the cosmos is totally unpredictable.

Science has always looked upon the universe as a gigantic clockwork, ticking through eternity in serene, predictable order. But Wisdom and Sussman, and growing ranks of their colleagues at the cutting edge of physics today, are seeing something else. While empirical laws of motion, entropy, gravitation, and other Newtonian constructs can lead to predictable patterns, increasingly they are seen to be spinning off into random anti-patterns, or chaos. How order and chaos can coexist is a problem science is just beginning to address, but Kabbalah has had the answer for millennia.

It is as simple as the difference between light and darkness, good and evil, positivity and negativity. In short, metaphorically speaking, order is the Light of the Creator, emanating from the Tree of Life, and chaos, spawned by the Tree of Knowledge, is the direct result of the massive disconnectedness of mankind.

Our minds boggle at the prospect that a complex system of atoms, swimming in primal chaos, can result in the orderly functioning of such a creature as a human being. How can stable patterns of behavior and physicality arise from a fundamentally chaotic world? The reality—the true reality—is that atoms do not swim in chaos. Their internal mechanisms and the energy and power they display, originate within the Spiritual Light where chaos does not exist.

For an example of this, one need look no further than the human heart. Traditional science treats this vastly complex system as though it were little more than a pump, the intricate cycles of which can be broken down into simple waves of standard frequency. But we all understand that the heart is more complicated than that. The heartbeat is pulsed by minute electronic signals from the brain, and the actual rhythmic contractions are the result, not of simple muscle tissue, but of billions of fibers, all working together in flawless harmony. When scientists conclude that this intricate, complex web of interactions could be operated by chaotic internal dynamics, we must then assume that science is no longer the study of existence, but that existence determines the results of scientific study.

To conclude, as science does, that atoms, molecules, and cells do not know that the heart they comprise beats is to be utterly unreasonable. There is consciousness—and a desire to receive—on every level of Creation, from a human being to a stone. There is a dynamic interplay occuring within a stone, interplay in which billions of atoms operate in harmony to keep it together. An incredibly wide array of minute, but conscious, movements occur within our own bodies as well, movements that reveal the infinity of the divine Light. And like the Light, we operate with a fundamental objective to share, and thus do good.

Microcosm and Macrocosm

To first understand and then control what the universe presents, we must come to understand the Tree of Life—a lineage that can represent the energy of a single human being or of the entire universe.

At first glance, you may be tempted to regard the schematic of the Tree as not much more than lines on paper, so simple is its design. Yet, it is a living, breathing metaphor that constricts and controls the awesome raw power of the Light of Creation. This Light can be used by anyone to achieve any positive thing, from healing of disease to acquisition of wisdom, love, and prosperity.

Science has known for some time that nothing exists in the universe except energy; Kabbalah takes that assertion one step further, holding that the energy of consciousness is all that really exists. Matter is merely an illusion. Our bodies and the most common material goods we acquire to benefit them can be turned back into energy in a flash of fire or a nanosecond of nuclear fusion.

The Tree of Life, with its ten Sfirot—or quantum packets of conscious, intelligent, energy—is distributed on the three columns as displayed in the diagram. It represents eternal life—the universe within and without—the only reality in existence.

The Ten Sfirot

The Sfirot embody many more elements than will be discussed here, but we start with the essential characteristics and attributes of the ten as they apply in the world in which we dwell.

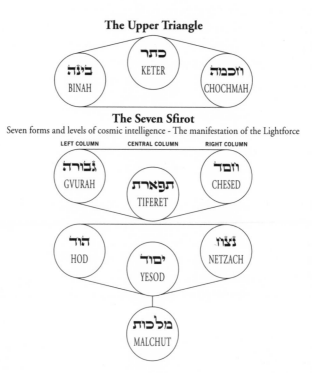

The Upper Triangle

כתר
KETER

בינה
BINAH

וזכמה
CHOCHMAH

The Seven Sfirot
Seven forms and levels of cosmic intelligence - The manifestation of the Lightforce

LEFT COLUMN   CENTRAL COLUMN   RIGHT COLUMN

גבורה
GVURAH

תפארת
TIFERET

וזסד
CHESED

הוד
HOD

יסוד
YESOD

נצח
NETZACH

מלכות
MALCHUT

The Sfira of Keter, which sits like a crown at the top of the Tree, above the central column, contains all the incarnations of all the souls in existence. It embodies God as unknown and unknowable and is located just below the endless world of limitless Light, far, far beyond mortal comprehension.

Keter is the blazing intelligence that channels the Light of the Creator to the rest of the Tree. It functions as a supercomputer, containing the total inventory of what each of us is, ever has been, or ever will be. As such, it is the genesis not only of our lives in this earthly realm, but of every thought, idea, or inspiration we ever will have while we sojourn here, and that includes lifetimes of the past, the present, and the future.

Keter is the source of everything, but only in an undifferentiated potential. The rest of the energy centers on the Tree of Life are needed to turn that potential into something we can perceive as reality.

The Sfira of Chochmah is the first center to receive the power flowing out of Keter. At the top of the right-hand column, Chochmah is the repository of all the wisdom in the universe and stands as the universal father figure.

Chochmah is the primordial point of Creation from which all knowable reality originates. It contains the totality of the Light. But wisdom, existing passively in a kind of warehouse, is of no value on any plane. To be of use, it must be inventoried, shipped out, and supplied to those in need of it. To accomplish that, Chochmah requires connection with its corresponding mother figure, which is the Sfira of Binah.

The Sfira of Binah, at the top of the left-hand column, represents understanding. Binah is a powerhouse of cosmic energy. It is the universal mother figure.

As Chochmah encapsulates all wisdom, Binah contains all energy, ranging from that which motivates human endeavor to that which keeps galaxies spinning. When thought must be made manifest in action, Chochmah and Binah meet. They combine their energies, filter them through "the invisible Sfira," otherwise known as Daath, or knowledge, and take this new energy to the next sphere, called Chesed.

The Sfira of Chesed, the most expansive of the Sfirot, sits below Chochmah on the right-hand column and represents mercy.

Chesed holds the still-undifferentiated seed of all that has taken place between Chochmah and Binah, and since it represents the total desire to share, it can be generous to a fault.

We all have seen Chesed run amok. It is the ultra-liberal who weeps more for the criminal than for the victim; it is the parents who cannot ever bring themselves to discipline their children. Fortunately, Chesed does have a balancing counterpart, just across the way, on the left-hand column, right under Binah. It is called Gvurah.

The Sfira of Gvurah represents judgment. If Chesed is like Charlie Chaplin's Little Tramp, who gallantly lays down his coat on a muddy street only to cause a fine lady to fall down a sewage hole, Gvurah is Ebeneezer Scrooge. Where Chesed expands, Gvurah contracts. Where Chesed says, "Share," Gvurah says, "What's in it for me?" Where Chesed forgives and forgets, Gvurah is a strict and wrathful disciplinarian. Gvurah, run amok, without Chesed's balance, becomes the tyranny of a police state.

But even as Chochmah's wisdom cannot become manifest without Binah's energy, neither can the undifferentiated seed that lies in Chesed ever become manifest without Gvurah's strong hand. That which Chochmah and Binah have passed down to Chesed, Gvurah brings into differentiation, which is the beginning of physicality. This process is not as complicated as it might sound and will be explained in detail in subsequent chapters.

The Sfira of Tiferet, representing beauty, or the ideal balance of justice and mercy, rests below Keter on the central column, and beneath Chesed on the right and Gvurah on the left. Tiferet is the balancing point between right and left columns, and without the symmetry of balance, there can be no beauty.

It is here, in Tiferet, that the wisdom of Chochmah and the understanding of Binah combine in the potential of Chesed and the manifestation of Gvurah to create the actuality that ultimately will be seen in our world. Tiferet is beauty, and like the things we call beautiful in this realm—a sunset, a poem, a flower, or a soul—Tiferet combines wisdom, understanding, and the luminosity of the Light.

The Sfira of Netzach, or victory, resides on the right-hand column, just below Chesed. A repository of positive energy from Chesed, Netzach radiates the desire to share and becomes the channel of that energy as it approaches the physical world in which we live.

It is, in short, analogous to the sperm that, in union with the egg, ultimately creates the individual human being. Netzach is also known as eternity, and it represents involuntary processes as well as the right brain, where the creative process takes place. Netzach, in short, is the artist, the poet, the musician, the dreamer, and the masculine fertilizing principle. Its feminine counterpart, directly across the way on the left-hand column, is Hod.

The Sfira of Hod, or glory, is analogous to the egg in human conception, and is also associated with prophecy. Hod begins the materialization of that which was held solely in potential in the male aspects of Chesed/Netzach. Hod also controls the voluntary processes and left-brain activities, channeling the practicality of Gvurah into the human psyche. As Netzach is the artist, Hod is the scientist, the logician, the math whiz, and the certified public accountant.

The Sfira of Yesod, or the foundation, sits like a great reservoir at the bottom of the Tree of Life. All the Sfirot above pour their intellect and their attributes into its vast basin where they are mixed, balanced, and made ready for transfer.

All the conscious actions that will be available to the Kabbalist—the thought, the energy, the intent, and the direction—are collected here in a radiance so brilliant no mortal could survive in its presence. As Binah is the generator of the source contained in Keter, Yesod is the generator of the destination, which is Malchut.

The Sfira of Malchut, the kingdom, contains the world of physicality. Think of Malchut as a house that Chochmah conceived, Binah provided the energy to build, Chesed imagined with love, Gvurah imagined with cold practicality, Tiferet actualized in a drawing, Netzach provided with color and ornamentation,

Hod cost-estimated, and for which Yesod shipped out the building materials.

Malchut houses the world in which we live. It is the only one of the Sfirot on the Tree of Life where physical material seems to exist in a minuscule percentage of the whole and where the Tree of Knowledge sinks its roots. And it is here that a divergence in human attitude spells the difference between individual lives lived in the Light and those lived in darkness.

Returning to the Tree of Life

Reincarnation, in which the human soul returns to this realm again and again until its karmic imperfections are corrected, is another central tenet of Kabbalah. This process, in which a soul is channeled down through the Tree of Life to be born in the physical portion of Malchut, begins in Keter, and no soul leaves there without the debts it has accrued in previous lifetimes. You might think of this as spiritual baggage. Unlike the luggage that winds up in Bangkok when you deplane in New York, your spiritual baggage always arrives at its proper destination. You couldn't lose it in transit if you wanted to. The sole purpose of your journey here is to leave your karmic baggage here in this realm when once again it is time to pass through the illusory door called death and return to the Tree of Life reality.

Most souls can lose their self-imposed burdens of karmic debt only through repeated trips to this plane of existence. For the Kabbalist, there is a powerful shortcut that will be revealed in chapter 5. For the moment, suffice it to say that the Light of Keter has a long way to go before it reaches us. It is as far removed from our physical realm as an architect's first thought is from the building he will eventually create.

The Tree of Knowledge

The Zohar states that humans and the cosmos are mutually supportive and inseparable aspects of the one all-embracing unified whole of reality. Negative energy-intelligence has been humankind's trademark since the fall of Adam, which is why we have trouble understanding the universal chaos.

We have always confused processes and origins, symptoms and causes. Instead of asking why illness, pollution, world wars, global financial depressions, and misfortunes occur, and trying to remove the conditions leading to them, we try to understand the problems themselves, focusing on how we can control violence, on how we can control illness. Thus politicians and governments, blind to the origins of disorder and conflict, con-centrate on the external—the visible acts of crime and violence —rather than on the deeper, metaphysical elements that give birth to these problems.

Out of this perversion rises the Tree of Knowledge, in many ways the antithesis of the Tree of Life, but its reflection nonetheless. The Tree of Knowledge is not, in itself, evil, though all evil stems from its left-hand column where chaos is born out of the desire to receive for the self alone. This desire, as we will see, is a short circuit of our divinely endowed ability to truly receive.

As a result of this short circuit, Maxwell's Second Law of Thermodynamics, otherwise known as the Law of Entropy, continues to dominate our existence. It states that the cosmos is in an irreversible state of decay—a winding down that is the very essence of chaos. Yet, while everything around us seems to point to eventual disintegration, it is still impossible to be sure that no order is possible in the universe. Science cannot say with absolute certainty that the universe began with the Big Bang, or whether it was born out of a random motion of atoms, or even if there exists an as-yet undiscovered arrangement among atoms. If atoms are in fact moving in a prearranged pattern to a common end, then cosmic collapse and decay need not occur.

The three parallel universes—the Tree of Life and the good and bad sides of the Tree of Knowledge—provide complete understanding of the contradictory features of the Law of Entropy. Without proper guidelines, humankind is destined to be controlled by the features of a chaotic universe subject to all the rules of entropy. Most of us spend our lives bouncing back and forth between the good and the bad sides of the Tree of Knowledge reality. We grasp things for ourselves alone in one moment, and share with others in another moment. The constant back-and-forth eventually just wears us out.

But if we can learn the methodology by which we can inhabit the Tree of Life, then decay and disintegration cannot invade our lives. Living fully under the Tree of Life, all physical matter, including that which constitutes our bodies, does not decay. Death—a random phenomenon belonging to the Tree of Knowledge—can never occur.

One cannot discuss the Tree of Knowledge without acknowledging the serpent who led Eve to its "forbidden fruit" in the story of Eden. The serpent of Genesis still is with us, and while this implacable enemy of humankind cannot enter the Tree of Life, he sits in his dark cosmic basement with headset on and tape recorder running; he has the Tree of Life "bugged," metaphorically speaking, all the way up to Keter. He has tapped into all the telephone lines in the universe, and he is aware, long before we are, of what is coming down through metaphysical channels for each of us. And while this adversary cannot affect that which is moving toward manifestation from Chesed through Yesod, he can seize and distort energy for us when it reaches his realm, here, in Malchut.

In this book, you will learn how to fight the serpent and win, but first this master of chaos must be exposed and defined so we will know exactly what we are up against in the battle to come.

Freedom from Chaos

There are, in essence, three parallel universes to which we have access: the Tree of Life, and the two aspects—one good and one evil—of the Tree of Knowledge. Metaphorically, Adam and Eve were forbidden to eat the fruit of the Tree of Knowledge in the Garden of Eden because then they would know the difference between good and evil. Once humans were able to make that distinction, paradise was lost.

And what, exactly, does "good" mean in this context? It has to do with Yesod consciousness, which immunizes against chaos. The Zohar explained it some 2,000 years ago by explicating the Bible verse, "Trust in the Lord and do good, dwell in the land, delight and pasture in Emunah."

Emunah, drawn from the word "amen," is the point at which the Tree of Life connects with and influences the Tree of Knowledge. The Zohar says one who clings to supernal Emunah is connected with the Light of the Creator and that, therefore, "no one in the entire world can cause harm unto him."

According to the Zohar, when you perform a good deed "below" (in Malchut) you arouse corresponding elements "above" in the Tree of Life. "Then," says the Bible, "you may dwell in the land with confidence, eat its fruit, and delight in it."

If, however, a person does not arouse cosmic forces above by positive actions below, then he or she will be distanced from those cosmic forces. The verse, "What shall we eat in the seventh year?" is answered by another verse: "I will shed my blessing upon you in the sixth year . . . See that the Lord giveth you on the sixth day the bread of two days."

The language carries an archaic ring, but its truth is as valid today as it was when it was written millennia ago. It has been understood since the invention of agriculture that fields left fallow in the seventh year of a planting cycle benefit from the rest and produce even heavier crops in subsequent plantings. The Zohar, however, connects the sixth year to the highly infused immune system of cosmic Yesod, and by so doing, reveals a new and different perspective. Once decoded by the Zohar, the biblical code takes on additional meaning. "What shall we eat in the seventh year?" means "How are we to deal with the problems of chaos and disorder in the seventh realm of existence?" which is Malchut, the mundane reality of our lives. The Bible promises that on the sixth day, "the Lord giveth you . . . the bread of two days," which means simply that Yesod is available to carry one through the "famine" of the seventh day.

When we connect with Yesod and do good, we activate the Sfira so that "no one in the entire world can cause any harm." In short, because whatever we do here is directly reflected above, we can rest in the seventh year—symbolized by Malchut—free of chaos and disorder, illness or financial instability.

Proactivity and Reactivity

The Light of the Tree of Life, which is to say God or the Creator, has no desire to receive that which He has invested in us. We are capable of experiencing the desire to receive in a holy or in an unholy way. The desire to receive for the sake of sharing is perhaps best characterized by a woman who receives a man's seed in order to give birth and nurture life. This kind of receiving is expressed in proactivity and, consequently, what we term "good." Those who become proactive, rather than reactive, initiate their own thinking and control their own emotions.

A desire to receive for the self alone, which lies like a black hole at the core of the Tree of Knowledge, creates reactivity and thus becomes the root of evil. The reactive personality lives a life with buttons on display for every passing stranger to push.

By way of example, picture those people who are told that a friend has insulted them. If they harbor a desire to receive for the self alone, they will be infuriated by this information; it conflicts with their emotional need to be constantly rewarded, complimented, and fulfilled. They will confront the friend angrily, possibly even threaten to "punch the friend's lights out" (a good Kabbalistic phrase, incidentally). This is a reactive action, the result of a prickly ego and a lack of self-confidence.

Though in the short run such people may seem to prosper, in the long run they will have nothing. By wanting everything for themselves, they restrict nothing and share nothing, thus shutting off the all-inclusive Light.

But for those whose desire to receive for the sake of sharing, there is no lack that needs fulfilling. An insulting remark will not send these people into paroxysms of anger. Such people have control over their emotions. Such people become proactive—so firmly grounded in a sense of worth that they will see the insult has nothing to do with themselves. Automatically, through a conscious act of sharing, in this case sharing their own beneficence with the offensive party, they establish an affinity with the Light and become at one with God.

Receiving and Sharing

And what, exactly, is sharing? Some in our society have been reared to believe that all material wealth somehow is sinful, and that in order to be "right with God" they must give it all away. Such a belief is a corruption of truth, designed by evil people whose only desire is to fleece their flocks and fatten their own purses. The Creator's sole desire is to share His beneficence; to give away all that we receive from Him is to reject Him and all that He would give us. A good rule of thumb in sharing anything—whether to charity or tithing to a church or synagogue—is this: Never less than 10 percent nor more than 20 percent. All things must be kept in balance.

Balance is impossible to achieve when a human circuit is plugged into the desire to receive for the self alone. In any such thought, action, or circumstance, the Light of the Creator is imprisoned—held, as it were, in a state of suspended animation. Simply put, a desire to receive for the self alone is a rejection of His beneficence, a restriction of His Light. God is in prison, and only we can free Him. There are specific and powerful meta-physical means available to this end that will be discussed in subsequent chapters, but in general, any conscious act of sharing breaks open the prison door and releases spiritual Light as surely as an exploding stick of dynamite will free the atoms immediately surrounding it into the atmosphere.

The first reactive impulse for anyone suddenly slapped in the face—literally or figuratively—is to lash back at the tormentor. But the proactive response says, "I want to assault this person, but I will not do what I want to do." That is restriction, or tak-ing control of your emotions, and in taking control, you become God, creating your own soul's destiny. Paradoxically, this restriction releases the spiritual energy within.

When by blessing or deed, you release spiritual Light from the place in which it is bottled up, you release yourself as well. Proactive people are passive people—they are simply immune to the pain of a slap, the fury of harsh words, or the oppression of a tyrant because their lives contain no dark corners in which such negative things can lodge.

Living in Light

But there is more to it than that. Upon Creation we were imbued with the essence of the Creator. Because of our shame, what Kabbalists call the Bread of Shame response to His beneficence, the Creator restricted His Light. And so we must, in turn, restrict our desire to receive in order to free Him and flood the physical universe with His Light. Because we were created in His image, we are charged to do more than merely worship God. We are God, and we must act accordingly.

Without the structure of circuitry provided by the Tree of Life and unlocked by Kabbalah, however, we can no more control the undiluted force of the Creator than we can handle a charge of raw current from a nuclear power plant. As with domestic electricity, spiritual Light must be scaled down to a level at which we can connect without killing ourselves. Still, we must have the means of tapping it if we are not to live in darkness.

Living in Light—the Light of the Creator—is what this book is all about. It will explain why, though a universe of Light is available to all of us, most of us stubbornly hide ourselves in a tiny corner of darkness. It will reveal levels of consciousness never even suspected. And, it will examine the phenomenon by which, though we may spurn the very thought of a supreme Creator as a reality in our lives, we nonetheless deify other "gods"— from the hero-warriors of basketball, baseball, hockey, and other modern versions of the battlefield, to movie stars and television actors—whether or not they have anything to celebrate.

This book also will serve as a road map to lead us out of this morass of uncertainty and illusion. As you will see, the road no longer lies exclusively in the realm of the metaphysical. At long last, science is catching up and showing the way, and its ultimate unfolding, called the "grand unified theory" by some, the "theory of everything" by others, is finally at hand.

CHAPTER 2

ADVERSARIES AND ALLIES

The only thing necessary for the triumph of evil is for good men to do nothing.

—*Attributed to Edmund Burke, 1729–1797*

The Opponent

He is known by many names: Lucifer, Prince of Darkness, Father of Lies, Old Scratch, the Devil, the Dark Lord . . . and, Murphy, as in Murphy's Law. Murphy's Law states that what can go wrong, will go wrong, and that if one of several things does go wrong, it will be the one bearing the worst consequences.

In Kabbalah, the Murphy mind-set represents a powerful force, a force that exists so that we can resist it, and build spiritual muscle in so doing. For that reason, we think of Murphy as the Opponent, or even as the Satan. Please note that Kabbalists refer to "the Satan" not simply "Satan" and the word is pronounced with the accent on the second syllable, to rhyme with rattan.

The Opponent lives in darkness and thrives on chaos. He is the motivating force behind all human ills, from war and mass murder to drug abuse, broken diets, and consistent failure to carry out the trash. We know we shouldn't, but the Opponent whispers, "Do it." We know we should, but the Opponent whispers, "Don't." The snake who visited Eve in the Garden of Eden was no snake at all. He was a lost angel called the Satan, an angel in whom all the negative energy in the world is rooted. Once the Satan whispered in Eve's ear, the negative energy entered her being and became a part of human nature, a part of us. The Opponent, therefore, is both outside of us and within us, and we surely sense his presence all too often.

Those who whine that "the Devil made me do it," are not entirely off base, except that the Opponent lacks the power to make anybody do anything.

The Opponent appears to rule the world, but he has a dirty little secret—one he desperately does not want his human foils to learn. The Opponent is an illusion. He is an extension of rational consciousness emanating from the Tree of Knowledge. His "law" works only because we accept and acknowledge it, and every time one of us acts upon an impulse to receive for the self alone, the spiritual energy we reject goes straight to the Opponent. Even the Opponent must eat, and the only way we'll ever get rid of him is to keep the energy for ourselves and starve him to death. The Opponent is the only entity in the universe with which we should not share.

Throughout the world of Malchut, the darkness of the Opponent lurks in a scant one percent of the physical spectrum, while the Light of the Creator, streaming from the Tree of Life, fills the remaining 99 percent. Some individuals harbor more darkness than others, and while a handful are so imbued with darkness as to have no souls at all, the vast majority of the Creator's created vessels hold about the same ratio of light to darkness as the rest of the universe. That leaves a minuscule 1 percent for the Opponent. We are that close to Paradise. Yet almost without exception, we turn away from the Light and dwell right where the Opponent wants us to dwell—in that 1 percent that constitutes the heart of darkness.

Living in the Material World

It should be easy to turn from the 1 percent to the 99 percent. But, as with all things involving the Opponent, there is a problem with the cure. We live in a universe that is 1 percent matter, the rest being energy. We cannot eradicate the material world, even though it is the only place in the cosmos where the Opponent holds sway. We therefore must dematerialize the Opponent without dematerializing the world in which we live.

We can do this by converting the desire to receive for the self alone to a desire to receive for the sake of sharing. That is the bedrock of Kabbalah, and it will be achieved through meditation techniques that will be revealed in the next chapter. But until we accomplish this metamorphosis, the Opponent will continue to rule our lives and punctuate the world with waves of war, crime, intolerance, hatred, hypocrisy, and ill will.

But how does the Opponent manage to lead men and women—even those with the highest intelligence and the best of intentions—to spread chaos throughout the cosmos by their negative actions?

Often, all that's required is simple passivity. Not speaking up— doing nothing in the face of evil—is what activates the Opponent. When actively challenged—when he's told he will not be tolerated—he cringes and fades away. But ignore him (or worse, deny his existence), and he has his way. Even though he, himself, is an illusion, he will lead those he has duped into the fragmentation of everything around them, including their own shattered lives.

Human action, within the circuit of Kabbalah, throws the switch on the Opponent and floods him with the Light he cannot bear. Unfortunately for the human race, he is rarely challenged, so his dark illusion and the chaos it fosters remains, in the lives of individuals and in the destinies of nations. But there is a way to beat the Opponent—a simple, down-to-earth, practical way, which is what this book is all about.

Shechinah, Our Spiritual Shield

Just as the Opponent is a built-in danger, there exists as well a natural protection, a kind of spiritual ozone layer called the Shechinah. Like her physical counterpart, she shields us from the harmful effects, not of the sun, but of the dark. But we must know how to summon her help. Her access password number, in fact, is a combination of Hebrew letters that constitute both the DNA code of the universe and everything in it, and the infinite gateways that offer all of us entry into the Tree of Life reality.

The means by which we summon the Shechinah against the Opponent is Kabbalistic meditation, the all-important bridge by which humankind finally will achieve a world without chaos. But first, let us get to know our protector.

The Zohar states that in every case, from the personal to the universal, chaos can be attributed to a key operative on the payroll of the Opponent, a malevolent energy intelligence called klippah. Klippah, which means husk, or covering, has as its objective the destabilization of the natural laws of balance. Klippah trips us up simply by getting in the way, blocking the Light, and keeping it from penetrating and influencing our environment.

When the Light of the Creator no longer pervades our universe, the klippah, whose familiar habitat is darkness, has dominion over everything. Thus, certainty is replaced with uncertainty, stability with imbalance, dependability with unaccountability, and decisiveness with indecision. In this fashion, its effect becomes manifest as illness, hatred, financial ruin, and violence of every description.

The Zohar is our guide to eliminating the klippah, and the Opponent's reign, from our lives. The Zohar says that we cannot wage war against the Opponent alone, as individuals. We have neither the power nor the means, and any such undertaking would be an exercise in futility. At best it would be like the forcible elimination of political and personal tyrants, which has never been a durable solution. New tyrants will always come forward to cause us misfortune.

Instead, the remedy is to let spiritual Light infiltrate our environment. Rather than attempt to remove the cancer of darkness by surgery, we must infuse it with Yesod consciousness by pervading the cosmos with the balanced immune system represented by that Sfira. To achieve a permanent solution, the Zohar considers it necessary to launch an attack upon the origin of chaos, which is the dark energy that surrounds klippah. In short, we must turn on the Light.

The Power of the Light

The Light sought here, and that the Kabbalah makes available, is more, by far, than any human can handle. It emanates from Yesod and it burns in the metaphysical firmament of the Tree of Life with the intensity of a star blazing in the physical cosmos of the Tree of Knowledge. The energy of Yesod, unfiltered, would vaporize us in an instant, just as it will also vaporize the evil husks of klippah, if we can get it there.

Enter the Shechinah, the liaison between the terrestrial realm of the Tree of Knowledge and the universe of Light that is the Tree of Life. In any situation, the Shechinah can be called upon to seize the klippah and transport it directly into the blazing heart of Yesod, there to be consumed once and for all. And make no mistake, that vaporization is permanent—Yesod has no use for temporary solutions. Every fragment of klippah that we destroy reduces the darkness at levels from the personal to the cosmic, advancing the day when the Opponent will be little more than an unpleasant memory.

Shechinah was there, along with Yesod, in the desert of Genesis, when Moses first encountered the Creator, and the Creator said, "You cannot see My face, for a man cannot see Me and live."

And the Lord said: "Behold, there is a place by Me, and you shall stand upon the rock. And it shall come to pass, while My glory passeth by, that I will put you in a cleft of the rock, and will cover you with My hand until I have passed by. And I will take away My hand, and you shall see My back, but My face shall not be seen."

The passage, of course, is a metaphor; the Creator has no face, back, or hand in the human sense. But the face spoken of here represents the very real power of the Light of the Creator, and the hand that covered Moses to keep him from being vaporized by that power is the Shechinah. The Shechinah can be called upon to operate for us in the same fashion today.

One clear objective in Kabbalistic meditation is to create communion with the Shechinah, making it serve as an intermediary, adapting and adjusting Yesod consciousness to the corporeal nature of our physical being. By this means, all of humankind can venture into the mysterious realm of the metaphysical forces that manage the dynamic interplay of our universe. It is our way in, our pathway to peace, our road map to a solution.

But, as the biblical metaphor makes clear, an approach to Yesod is not without peril. If we are to tap the spiritual energy of Yesod consciousness, we must be extremely careful that proper safeguards are taken so as to prevent burnout or violent reaction. We must never come in direct contact with the invisible expressions of the Light. As the ozone layer acts as a filter shielding us from an excess of ultraviolet radiation, so does the Shechinah filter and modify the Light of the Creator so that it will be bearable to us.

Keep It Joyful

Kabbalah offers no one a free lunch. Its benefits are vast, but they must be worked for with study, practice, and above all, attitude. The Shechinah is, after all, a child of the spiritual Light, and like a child, its attributes are trust and an utter lack of doubt and negativity. The Shechinah will function against darkness, but not in darkness. The mind of the practitioner who wishes to summon the Shechinah must be free and clear of all gloom, grief, disbelief, or depression.

The Bible provides a parable, a metaphorical example in the story of Joseph.

Jacob, the founding patriarch of Israel, loved his son, Joseph, ahead of all his other sons because Joseph was the offspring of Rachel. Jacob, you may remember, had worked for Rachel's father, Laban, for seven years on the promise of her hand in marriage. But, Laban cheated him, marrying him off to Rachel's sister, Leah, instead. Jacob was so smitten with Rachel that he willingly put in another seven years of indentured servitude so that he could marry her as well.

Jacob's devotion to Joseph left a bad taste in the mouths of Joseph's ten elder siblings. Finally, after enduring their father's overt favoritism for years, the sons of Jacob seized their younger half brother, imprisoned him in a pit (a metaphor, incidentally, for the klippah), and sold him into slavery. To cover up their crime, they told Jacob his beloved son had been killed by wild animals—a lie that plunged Jacob into a grief as deep as death. As the Lord's chosen, Jacob always had maintained constant contact with the Light, through the Shechinah, but when gloom swallowed him, the Shechinah departed, leaving him in darkness for 17 years until Joseph's triumph in Egypt reunited them.

The Zohar states: "The Shechinah does not rest where there is defect, but only in a place where there is wholeness, not in a place where lack exists, nor where grief is present, but only in a place of correctness and joy. Therefore, all the years that Joseph was separated from his father, and Jacob was in grief, the Shechinah did not rest upon him."

Not even the patriarch could live in the Light while he lived in grief. So, the next time someone tells you to "let it go" or to "have a nice day," don't take umbrage. No matter how trite it may sound, this is excellent advice.

Even with a positive attitude, however, there are three months of the year in which the Shechinah is not available to us. There are some complicated metaphysical reasons for this departure but, for the present, let us just say that like any good civil servant, the Shechinah lists vacation time among its job benefits. Its holidays are the Hebrew months of Tevet, astrologically ruled by the sign of Capricorn; Tammuz, under Cancer; and Av, dominated by Leo. These months fall roughly from the first week of December to the first week of January, the second week of June until the second week of July, and the last week of July to the last week of August, respectively. Actual dates vary from year to year, but when these dates occur, we are left without protection. Unless we construct our own security shields, at these times we stand in grave danger of being burned by the unfiltered Light.

We can build our own personal version of Shechinah through increased practice of restriction, meditation, and fasting and by keeping to the "shade" of limited activity. In months in which the Shechinah is taking a break, it is not a good idea to launch ambitious new projects, either of a personal or a business nature.

Now that you know the Shechinah, what its powers are, and what it stands ready to do for you, it is time to explore the means of harnessing it. The means actually are simple, but never confuse "simple" with "simple-minded." The complex, layered, intricate universe can and must, from the Kabbalistic point of view, be brought to the level of extreme simplicity, which is the chief stumbling block encountered by people first discovering Kabbalah. We have been programmed to believe that our affairs are too complex to be resolved with easy, simple solutions; we are predisposed not to believe in simplicity. Let that doubt be banished now.

You are about to learn about the letters of power. Their combinations form the 72 Names of God and the most powerful prayers ever devised. You are about to learn how to arrange those letters for specific purposes, how to scan them for effect, and how to meditate upon them for healing and travel through space. You are about to learn how to roll any entity or situation back from its "real" to its potential state, to eradicate any evil aspect that might be invading your life.

In short, you are about to learn how to evict the Opponent, take control of your life, and live as you never have lived before. And you don't have to hold a PhD from MIT or Caltech to get the job done.

CHAPTER 3

SPIRITUAL TOOLS

My feet hurt and I got periodic bouts of depression, but other than that, I'm fine.

—*Roseanne Conner of Roseanne, upon being asked, "How are you?"*

Overcoming Chaos

Roseanne, of the eponymous ABC sitcom, had a lot of critics who would have liked to see life in America portrayed the way it was when Leave It to Beaver and Father Knows Best ruled the Nielsen ratings. The show may have gone off the air, but those critics are still fighting a losing battle. Roseanne—and the other dysfunctional families we see on TV—offer a truer picture of American life today.

In Roseanne's TV family, genuine love and devotion were constantly skewed by Murphy's dictum that what can go wrong, will go wrong. Raised by an abusive father and a mother with a tongue as sharp as a knife, Roseanne tried valiantly to eat her way—both metaphorically and literally—out of the frustration that clouded her life. Her husband struggled to maintain sanity from minute to minute, her sister raised promiscuity to an art form, her daughters fought, and her son, having transcended the bounds of mere weirdness, ate cardboard.

Roseanne may not have been politically correct, but people watched it because they recognized our reality in it. About 95 percent of American families are like hers to one degree or another. And, like the character Roseanne plays, most people have the innate comic buoyancy to bounce back from everyday blows and the innate joy to go on loving life.

There is hope for all the real-life Roseannes, trapped in short-term cycles of chaos filled with too little money and too many bills, sadistic bosses, feckless lovers, and the ever-present threat that an unpaid mortgage will leave the whole family homeless. This kind of chaos is the work of the Opponent, and only human consciousness and the power of the mind can bring lasting order out of chaos. Kabbalah can emancipate the mind of the individual and the collective mind of all civilization simply by liberating the energy packed into the individual letters of the Aleph Bet—the Hebrew alphabet and the building blocks of the universe and everything in it.

A preposterous statement? Not at all. "And the whole was of one language and of unity." That's how the Bible explains it in the story of the Tower of Babel in Genesis. Language—the Hebrew language to be specific—was created eons before the creation of Adam, long before there were any human creatures around to speak it or to read it. These 22 letters—as alive today as they were in the beginning—comprise the software by which the Creator created everything in existence, and by which we today can access the reality of the Tree of Life.

Moses, who used the Aleph Bet the way a computer whiz today uses complex codes, was capable of direct communication with the raw energy that is the Creator, any time necessity arose. Moses, alone, needed no Shechinah to intercede and shield him from the full power of the Light. No one since Moses has borne the full mantle of that power, but the coded language that Moses used remains a working system, and anyone who understands its use can tap its energy today.

Using the Tools

The first requirement for anyone who would enter the Tree of Life is to approach the problem with the desire to receive for the sake of sharing. Let us say that our hapless heroine has just made another inappropriate wisecrack and lost another job. The mortgage on her house is coming due and her husband, whose sole marketable skill is the ability to nail up drywall without making holes in it, hasn't worked for months. If the bulk of her concern genuinely lies with her husband and their children, all of whom stand to suffer if the house is lost, then her desire to retain it is based upon desire to receive for the sake of sharing.

Here are the tools such a person must muster if, having studied the Tree of Life sufficiently to understand the basics of its circuitry, she hopes to slip out of the Opponent's grasp and take control of her life. First, she must know precisely what it is she seeks from the beneficence of the Light. In this case, it is simply enough income to avert the present crisis. Then she needs the proper configuration of Hebrew letters, or one of the 72 Names of God, which, with their dominant characteristics, can be found in the chart on the following page.

One does not need to be able to read, or even pronounce, the Hebrew words that will provide the software for activating meditation. Their power lies within the shape of the letters.

One needs only to visualize them with intensity, to see them clearly even when the eyes are shut. With the basics assembled, we are now ready to embark. We are ready to make a minute alteration in consciousness that will allow us to depart from the fragmented noise and confusion of the Opponent and his Tree of Knowledge.

The 72 Names

כהת	אכא	ללה	מהש	עלם	סיט	ילי	והו
הקם	הרי	מבה	יזל	ההע	לאו	אלד	הזי
וזהו	מלה	ייי	נלך	פהל	לוו	כלי	לאו
ושר	לכב	אום	ריי	שאה	ירת	האא	נתה
ייז	רהע	וזעם	אני	מנד	כוק	להו	יוו
מיה	עשל	ערי	סאל	ילה	וול	מיכ	ההה
פוי	מבה	נית	גגא	עמם	הועש	דני	והו
מוזי	ענו	יהה	ומב	מצר	הרוז	ייל	נמם
מום	היי	יבמ	ראה	וזו	איע	מנק	דמב

The Green Light

Kabbalistic meditation is unlike any of the many forms that have swept the public consciousness in recent decades, from the transcendental variety of the 1970s to Silva mind control.

Those methods are useful in quieting the internal dialogue and in achieving relief from the stresses of the day, but they lack the powerful software of Kabbalah.

Meditation is like an automobile: it may be in good working order and have a full tank of gas, but in order to get it out onto the highway, you must know how to start the engine and put it in gear. Even that, however, is not enough if you do not know where you are going or how to get there. And even if you do know, the Opponent is very good at throwing up roadblocks at every intersection along the way—construction on this stretch, a broken water main over here. You are only trying to get to the bank to make a cash withdrawal, but after wasting time wandering around obstacles, you wind up at the local fast-food drive-in—which is fine if what you want is a hamburger and a cup of coffee. But the only money you will get there is your change.

With the Opponent at large, that metaphoric scenario happens frequently, which is one more reason why so many prayers go unanswered. But there is a way to beat the Opponent at his own game, and that is to climb into a metaphysical vehicle so advanced it makes a Lamborghini look like an Edsel. The name of this wondrous vehicle, which comes with a guarantee that it will skip over or fly around every barricade to prayer that the Opponent can erect, is Ana beko'ach, which will be discussed in full detail in chapter 5. You can get a test drive there, but for now, a bit more information on meditation and prayer is needed.

In Kabbalah, prayer and meditation are inextricably linked. Prayer without the intense concentration of Kabbalistic meditation is little more than a collection of words, while meditation without prayer is little more than a momentary palliative for stress. The most faithful practitioners of religion pray daily, though frequently in a robotic way, repeating words and phrases whose meaning they scarcely know. Such action has all the logic of a person who, upon discovering that he or she is running a high fever, picks up the telephone and calls a lawyer. As invaluable as a lawyer may be when there is a legal problem, it's the wrong number to dial when there is a health problem. That is why most prayers go unanswered.

It has been emphasized before that Kabbalah is not a religion, and the point must be reemphasized here. Religion, especially as practiced in its fundamentalist form, takes the Bible as a literal narrative of past events involving the relationship between God and humankind. The Kabbalist, however, sees something deeper in these tales. The Kabbalist sees in the Bible and in the letters of the Hebrew alphabet the underlying code for the meaning of existence and the essential principles that form our universe.

As a language, Hebrew loses almost everything in translation. Translations, in fact, have resulted in a shift from the metaphysical reality commanded by the letters to the metaphor of God on the physical plane, a phenomenon that early on introduced the idea of an anthropomorphic deity upon which all the great religions still are based.

The phrase, "and the Lord spoke to Moses," means something in Hebrew that is utterly lacking in translation to English or any other language in common use. "The Lord," in Hebrew, is not the stern old graybeard depicted by Michelangelo on the ceiling of the Sistine Chapel. He is pure, raw, naked energy, without physical form—a presence all-pervading throughout the universe.

But if the Creator is everywhere and anywhere, why can't we reach Him? Why do our prayers go unanswered? To find answers to these questions, people through the ages have looked deep within themselves in a desire to communicate with the Light of the Creator.

Light in the Night

Kabbalistic meditation techniques are more than just exercises. They employ a force called kavanah, without which there can be neither meditation nor prayer at any effective level. Like all Hebrew words, kavanah is tough to translate, emerging in various connotations as concentration, attention, intention, fervor, and devotion. But most of all, it stands for direction, and without the direction of kavanah, prayer and meditation are likely, at worst, to take practitioners nowhere in particular, or at best, to a location they really have no need or desire to reach.

Kavanah, then, is the driving force needed to keep a meditation on track and a prayer on target. In prayer, kavanah is the primary force, and the words of the prayer are only of secondary importance. Kavanah is the soul of the prayer, and the meditative construct of light within light is the manifestation upon which the necessary intense concentration can be focused.

The effects can be very powerful. Quantum physics tells us that the same electron can be at opposite ends of the universe. But the phenomenon of bilocation or even teleportation is by no means new to Kabbalists. They've been teleporting themselves for centuries with the "technology" of kavanah-driven meditation.

The first recorded event of such a teleportation is found in Genesis. Lot, the nephew of Abraham, was living in a very bad neighborhood—in fact, he was living in Sodom. Sodom was run by a mean-spirited bunch who, along with their other evils, had decreed death to anyone caught being nice to a stranger. And so Lot was being brave when, one night, he saw an amazing sight—two "angels" who showed up at the city gate—and he jumped up and ran to greet them. He did so, not out of contempt for the local law or out of awe for a vision of the Heavenly Host, but because the angels appeared to him in the form of his righteous uncle, Abraham, a man Lot knew was more than a match for any Sodomite thug.

Abraham was actually far, far away that night, but he also was there, in Sodom, to warn his wayward nephew that he had better pack up his family and get out of town before the sky fell in, which it did, shortly thereafter.

Things really haven't changed in the roughly 3,800 years since that drama was played out. Bilocation still works, because when we raise our consciousness by the process of meditation, we become aware that the only limits upon our corporeal bodies are those we have been programmed to believe exist. Without such limits, we literally can go wherever we wish to go, in real time, leaving our bodies in one spot while the true essence of our being is in another.

To do this, we need only to enter a meditative state, concentrate upon a selected destination, and then "see" ourselves standing there. If concentration is strong enough and the mind is silent enough to connect with the Light, we suddenly will experience the electrifying condition of being outside our body in the dual roles of observer and observed. This phenomenon is not unknown to modern quantum physics, and it also has been reported in hundreds of near-death experiences.

Dancing in the Light

Once we arrive at such a state, here is the scene that must greet the eyes of imagination if we are to proceed further:

Our body has been transformed into Light, as have all of our surroundings. In the center of our view is a throne of Light, above which is another Light called Nogah (glow). Facing the throne is yet another throne, above which there is a Light called Tov (good). We are standing between the two.

Now we notice even more illumination. To the right of Tov blazes another Light, called Bahir (brilliant), and to the left burns another, called Zohar (radiant). Above these two, and directly between them, is a Light called Kavod (glory). It is surrounded by another Light called Chaim (life), and above that sits a luminous crown. This crown contains all of the desires of the mind, illuminating the paths of the imagination. This Light has no end and cannot be fathomed, but from the glory of Kavod comes desire, blessing, peace, life, and all good to those who keep the way of its unification.

At this stage in the meditation, we have a choice. We can seek the mercy we need simply by turning to the right where the Tov of Chesed burns, there to speak the words to avert financial disaster. Or, if we feel the pressure of someone who seeks to harm us or any member of our family, we can turn to the left where the Nogah of stern Gvurah burns. Kabbalah cannot be used to inflict evil on others, but under the influence of Gvurah, which carries the qualities of restriction and judgment, we can remove evil caused by others. They will be stopped in their tracks and never know why.

There are other, even more powerful, meditative means to this end, and they will be detailed later. Suffice it to say that the effect of trying to use the Tree of Life for dark purposes can be the equivalent of sticking a finger into a plugged-in electrical socket. The energy coursing through the Tree of Life is no more judgmental than an electrical current. At 110 volts, the shock can be severe; at 220 volts, it can be fatal.

But there is not one among us who needs to wreak havoc on friends and family; thanks to the Opponent, that will happen without our help. So, after stating our need in the presence of Tov's Light, we must then superimpose upon that Light the Hebrew letters we have chosen to facilitate our quest and, concentrating upon them, allow our essence to rise toward the Light of Kavod, within the Light of Chaim.

All of this is going on deep within the confines of the mind. According to the strength of our concentration, we will be able to transmit power through desire, desire through knowledge, imagination through thought, strength through effort, and fortitude through contemplation to win the day.

With guidance and practice, communication with these sites can lead to a state of quiet never before imagined, but the image is not an easy one to maintain. Nor is successful teleportation yet common, even among those seriously studying Kabbalah. Never forget that while the Opponent may be an illusion, he still has the power to instill doubt. The Opponent does not want us in charge of our minds, bodies, and lives, and whenever we approach the means of achieving control through meditative teleportation, he starts planting the seeds of doubt.

"Don't be a fool," he whispers. "You know it doesn't work; have you ever seen it work? What will your friends and coworkers think if they find out you're seriously dabbling in this nonsense? The neighbors will be scandalized. Give it up and get serious."

The Opponent is very good at what he does, but with persistence, you can prevail. When his barrage of distraction and negativity hits you, relax with it. Whenever a negative thought pierces the meditative calm, stop the meditation process and patiently balance the imagery with a positive thought. Then return to the meditation, visualizing yourself once again at the center of the energy.

Charging the Batteries

There are powerful energy centers all over the globe, where the Light of the Creator is concentrated, that are the prime destinations in teleportation. There are many, scattered from Israel through Iraq, Iran, Morocco, the United States, and Canada. They are called holy sites because mystics, master Kabbalists, and righteous rabbis of years past are buried there. The sites are holy, not because the masters are there, but because the masters, knowing these particular sites were holy, chose them as their final resting places. They were, in effect, setting themselves up as lighthouses, marking power centers that have existed from the dawn of Creation, waiting for one whose consciousness has risen high enough to reveal them.

For the Kabbalist, the sites supercharge meditation, and the souls of saints interred there forever are available to provide strength, counsel, and intercession for those who know how to approach them. Rabbi Shimon bar Yohai, whose own resting place in Meron, in the Galilee, is one of the holiest of energy centers today, wrote of this 2,000 years ago when he said, "When the world is in distress, then one must go to the cemetery to offer supplication, where the dead then take note of the scroll (Torah). Then the soul goes and informs the Creator, who takes note and has pity on the world."

An indication of the importance of such holy sites is found in the Zohar's account of the passing of Rabbi Shimon. Knowing the power of Meron, he had selected that city as his final resting place, but so great was the Rabbi's renown that residents of nearby Tsepori were determined to see him interred there instead. The Zohar reports that they came in force to seize the body, triggering a riot as Meronites drove them away "with terrifying shrills and yelling."

People did not take such things lightly in Rabbi Shimon's day, and they are to be taken no less lightly now. Today, hundreds of thousands of pilgrims visit the burial site, as they have for two millennia, to connect with the energy of one who can only be called a holy luminary.

Jerusalem, the Destination

Of all the holy sites on Earth, the city of Jerusalem is the most powerful—and, for those who approach it in ignorance, the most dangerous. Jerusalem owes its original power to the way in which the Temple was constructed, and to the fact that the Ark of the Covenant was installed within its walls. The Ark was the instrument through which the supreme source of energy-intelligence was drawn. Today the Ark lives on in its present-day form—as scrolls in little "arks" in synagogues all over the world—and is still a device of staggering power. But there is more to it than that.

Though the original Ark disappeared when a Babylonian army sacked Jerusalem in 586 BCE, the Ark still exists. It is hidden within the Temple mount. The rebuilt Temple also still exists. Unfortunately, even if both were in plain view, no one could see them because the common consciousness of humankind assumes they are not there.

Today, the only visible construct of the Temple is the Wailing Wall. Even the Romans, though they certainly tried, were unable to pull it down. The sole purpose of the Temple was to harness the raw power of the Light, but with the Temple now beyond mass perception, Jerusalem remains a power station with its energy dangerously unharnessed, which is why more blood has been spilled in its streets than in those of any other city in the world. Metaphysically, Jerusalem is analogous to a nuclear plant that, after the fashion of Chernobyl, has suffered a core meltdown. In such a case, all who enter without protective anti-radiation gear are consumed. And, since the destruction of Solomon's Temple some 2,500 years ago, many have entered Jerusalem and perished.

Because of its immense power, great empires from the Babylonian to the British have coveted the city without even knowing why. One by one, having conquered just about everything else, they have been driven to make Jerusalem their final conquest and, one by one, they have fallen into ruin shortly thereafter. To seize Jerusalem, without understanding what it really is, is to seize disaster.

Other holy sites are not so dangerous, but to approach any of them without knowledge of their metaphysical power is, at best, futile. For those who know how to harness their power, however, the possibilities are limitless.

We are not restricted to the use of any single one of the world's known holy sites, but the mechanics of approach are the same for any of them. The sites have their own distinctive magnetic fields, which can be felt by those approaching them. It is most important that practitioners select a personal site with which they are thoroughly comfortable. Once there, they must begin meditation by reciting the 33rd Psalm, in Hebrew. Again, it is not necessary that the words be understood, only that they be correctly pronounced.

Doing the Math

Reasons for choosing the 33rd Psalm are complicated. They involve the assignment of numerical values to the letters of the text, a science that will not be deeply probed in this book since the subject could fill a volume of its own. Still, to give the student a taste of the massive sweep of Kabbalah, a brief explanation of the process is due.

The Zohar teaches that each of us has two bodies: an ethereal body of sharing and a second corporeal body given to receiving for the self alone. To communicate with the righteous, whose corporeal bodies do not decay in the grave (as the Nazis found to their astonishment when they exhumed some of them during World War II), we must achieve dematerialization of our second bodies. That is where Psalm 33 comes in.

This psalm consists of 22 verses, even as the Aleph Bet consists of 22 letters, and those 22 verses are comprised of 161 words. Again, never mind what the words mean; their purpose is to open a channel of communication with the Sfira of Binah, because that is the energy force capable of dematerializing the rational consciousness with its desire to receive for the self alone. For those with a mathematical bent, here is the formula:

The numerical value of 161 corresponds to the biblical code of Eyeh (104): Aleph (111), Hey (Hey + Yud = 15), Yud (Yud + Vav + Daled = 20). When the four-letter word Eyeh is spelled out as pronounced, the seed letters emerge as a dematerializing channel. When fully spelled out, the Aleph emerges as a three-letter structure, Aleph, Lamed, and Pey; the Hey emerges as a two-letter structure, Hey and Yud; the letter Yud emerges as a three-letter structure, Yud, Vav, and Daled; and the final Hey emerges as the first Hey (Hey and Yud). The numerical value of the composition expressed in the original coded formula of Eyeh thus adds up to 161—the number of words in Psalm 33.

Even if you flunked algebra and never really became comfortable with anything beyond long division, do not despair. Kabbalah has many levels and you do not need a PhD in Kabbalistic math to practice most of them, though without it, the full scope of the unseen forces woven so deeply into the fabric of our physical reality cannot be grasped. Suffice it to say that the mathematics of rational consciousness cannot reveal the full significance of the natural order of the universe. To the

Kabbalist, Kabbalistic mathematics is the language of nature itself.

There are, of course, other methods of connection with the Tree of Life reality that do not require the esoteric math of the numerological Aleph Bet. But Kabbalah is a daily discipline, and the practitioner must become so steeped in its general principles that no other existence is possible. It is not enough simply to read and talk about Kabbalah. One must do Kabbalah, and while the doing is not difficult, it must be done with vigor and consistency.

The Opponent Is a Hacker

The chart displaying the Hebrew letters forming the 72 Names of God is a good example of another powerful means of channeling spiritual Light.

One does not even need to achieve a deep meditative state in order to use it.

The individual names have powerful connotations for deep meditation and prayer, and taken together they can be used much as an anti-viral computer software is used. A computer virus (human-made or Opponent-made) can be picked up from a contaminated e-mail or even from an innocent stroll through the Web sites of the Internet. However contracted, the results can be devastating, with hard drive information utterly destroyed. Some have lost years of work to this vandalism.

To protect one's computer hard drive against such an assault, one uses antiviral software that, with the click of an icon, runs a full diagnostic of the system, quickly killing any virus it finds and clearing all applications for trouble-free use.

To protect his metaphysical hard drive, the Kabbalist uses the 72 Names of God. To prevent a chaos assault by the Opponent, all one has to do is scan the 72, from right to left, taking note only of the shapes of the letters, and the software is activated. As one concentrates upon each block, the letters actually seem to dance as they clear mind and soul of the virus of negativity.

Scrolling Up

There exists another, even more powerful, piece of antiviral software. This consists simply of the reading of the scroll of Torah each Sabbath in a Jewish synagogue. Most synagogues are open to all, so the gentile practitioner of Kabbalah willing to don a yarmulke out of respect for a house of worship will find himself welcome at the service.

Unfortunately, most Orthodox Jews who attend synagogue every Shabbat find very little comfort in their attendance, and the reading of the scroll offers few, if any, practical advantages or improvements in their personal lives. That is because they have forgotten (if ever they really knew) that the reading can reveal the highest, most potent spiritual Light. As a result, they pay no attention to what is going on. When the scroll is read, most congregants can be found in the midst of conversation about mundane matters of the day, while others simply take a break and leave the congregation hall.

Knowledge is connection, and the weekly reading of the Bible's coded message, when decoded by Kabbalah, makes that connection, with an effort no more strenuous than listening to the words.

The sages who divided the five books of Moses into weekly readings did not do so for congregants with limited attention spans. There are times when a single reading will involve 176 verses and other times when only 30 will be read. The scroll is shrouded in mystery, and the combination and number of verses in each reading constitute the interface between the universal hardware and the individual operating it through the software of the Aleph Bet. Get it wrong—read a section at an inappropriate time or drop a single word—and it will not work, any more than a computer program will work if the wrong disk or CD-ROM is inserted.

The more we become acquainted with the hidden messages of the weekly reading, the greater is our connection to the Light of the Creator, but a superficial translation can only encourage confusion in our lives. To make matters worse, the vast majority of scrolls in synagogues around the world are invalid. All it takes to render a scroll of Torah invalid is one dropped letter, one forgotten verse, or one misspelled word—deviations that can occur any time the mind of the scribe transcribing a scroll is elsewhere. In any other text, such errors could be written off as clumsy but relatively inoffensive typographical errors. But the scroll is a vehicle of pure spiritual Light, one deviation and the Light no longer can flow through its letters.

Even the physical condition of the scroll can affect its transmission capabilities. Just as a human being cannot function at full capacity if injured or ill, a single hairline crack in a single letter leaves a scroll unfit and unable to contain the full power of the Light. But a flawless scroll is an instrument of almost unimaginable metaphysical power.

The proper reading of a scroll works simply by activating another Kabbalistic principle that says there is no subdivision of time in the Tree of Life reality. When the scroll is being read, there is no yesterday, today, and tomorrow; all time is manifest in the here and now. The number of verses selected at the proper time apply to what the rational consciousness erroneously regards as the future. With that connection made, the "future" thus can be controlled today.

Each weekly scroll reading anticipates the chaos of the day and supplies the antidote seen in advance by the sages. In structuring the weekly reading, the sages also provided key words containing the same numerical value as the number of words being read. As a result, each week we are furnished with the information codes necessary to enhance the well-being of humankind. By thus connecting with the universal hardware of the Light of the Creator, we are supplied with the inoculation against the foreordained chaos and disorder of our lives.

The Opponent, of course, is delighted by the fact that few observant Jews now are aware of the power generated by a proper reading of the scroll, or that scrolls read in their own synagogues probably are flawed. He has managed to penetrate the deepest recesses of our minds and cloud them on this subject. Because the weekly reading of the scroll is more powerful than all of the other meditative equipment offered in this book, he may justifiably consider that act to be his best work.

But through Kabbalah, we have work of our own—work guaranteed to confound the Opponent and break his grip on our lives. Let us now explore the concept of a universe concealed within a seed.

CHAPTER 4

CHANNELS OF ENERGY

To see a world in a grain of sand and a heaven in a wild flower, To hold infinity in the palm of your hand and eternity in an hour.

—William Blake, 1757–1827

Everyday Miracles

The only thing more miraculous than what we hold to be miracles, are the miracles we take for granted, or worse, those to which we give no thought at all. Consider, for example, the apple seed.

What possible "miracle" might one find there? As seeds go, they aren't much. Tiny, dull colored, inedible, apple seeds are nothing more than unnoticed fragments, consigned to the garbage along with the core when the rest of the apple has been consumed. But consider this: one tiny, insignificant bit of botanical matter contains an entire apple tree—root, trunk, limb, branch, twig, leaf, and fruit, as well as DNA capable of producing all the apple trees that ever will exist. That's a pretty good performance for something no bigger than an ant.

As in keeping with the Kabbalistic tenet "As above, so below," the seed has a stunning counterpart within the Tree of Life. This counterpart is so powerful and so profound that were it to be utilized in full by the collective consciousness of humankind, we would be back in the Garden of Eden in a heartbeat.

The "seed" of everything in existence lies within Chesed on the right-hand column of the Tree of Life. There, all things, from atoms to galaxies, are held in an undifferentiated, potential state, just as the seed holds the entire apple tree. This should not be difficult to understand, especially if you consider that all human creative works begin in this fashion. The great novel, the magnificent painting, the revolutionary invention all begin with the seed of an idea, the dream of what the idea eventually will become.

But without human energy, the novel, the painting, and the invention never can become manifest. In the Tree of Life, energy is the provenance of the left-hand column. Only when the undifferentiated "seed" within Chesed is passed to Gvurah through the restrictive process of Tiferet, can it become the differentiated "tree" that can then bloom and bear its fruit here in Malchut.

It is easy to see that the human mind can learn to manipulate its own creative forces. The torrent of art, literature, and technological genius that has marked our brief passage here is all the proof required. But how can a human control and manipulate the creative forces of spiritual Light?

"As above, so below," there is no difference. Understand that the Kabbalist has it within his or her power to control and manipulate the Chesed-to-Gvurah process, even reversing it when circumstances demand that some material entity such as a cancerous tumor or a life-wrecking tragedy be "rolled back" from tree to seed and thus ejected from the physical world.

There is one mighty engine by which this "miracle" can be accomplished. It will be discussed more fully in the next chapter, but meanwhile, here are the ingredients and their potential uses.

Cell Renewal

Medical science tells us that every cell in the human body is replaced roughly every seven years—a proposition that would seem to imply an inborn "Fountain of Youth" guaranteeing that we remain forever young and forever free of disease and physical death. But no such extended warranty comes with these bodies we occupy. Like everything else in the universe of the Opponent, we are subject to entropy. But we do not have to be.

Cells that "die" do not cease to exist. Their atomic structures remain essentially unchanged in their undifferentiated state. Clipped fingernails and hair trimmed by the barber swiftly grow back, so why are such things as organ transplants and prosthetic devices still necessary? When a heart, a liver, or a lung become diseased, or when a limb is severed, why can't the person so afflicted simply grow a new one? The DNA that created it in the first place is still there. Why can one not simply call upon it to repeat the original creative process?

The answer, which may sound quite surprising, is that one can, if one is properly connected to the rejuvenation process.

These things will be covered in detail in subsequent chapters, but more immediately we must learn to use the process of turning undifferentiated seed potential into manifested physical reality by blessing the Lord to release spiritual energy and banking the positive moment against a rainy day of gloom and negativity. Neither is difficult and both are essential to happiness and well-being.

Banking on the Positive

There is an anonymous lament that ruefully observes, "When I'm right, nobody remembers; when I'm wrong, nobody forgets." The Opponent, of course, likes the concept. That way, even when he loses a round to a moment of good feeling and positive thinking on our part, he can win it back later when, as all mortal flesh must, we slip once again on a banana peel of negativity. If only we could retain or bank our positive energy—perhaps even in an interest-bearing account—to draw on when we are down and depressed!

The Zohar provides us with a methodology to set up just such a bank account of positive energy, energy designed to keep chaos out of our lives even when chaos seems to reign all around us. We open the bank account by means of a conscious act called blessing the Lord.

To a society accustomed to seeking blessing from the Lord, this may seem a strange concept. But Deuteronomy 8:10 says, "And you shall eat thereof, become satiated and bless the Lord." Note, the verse does not say "ask the Lord's blessing," or "ask the Lord to bless the food and drink He has given you for sustenance," though that is the common practice when religious people of nearly all persuasions say grace at the dinner table. The Zohar says the recipient of the Lord's bounty must bless Him "for the purpose of drawing the beneficence of Life from the source of Life." This concept is so important that the Zohar magnifies it, adding, "If one does not bless the Lord, then he is considered as having robbed the Lord."

But why should we bless the Lord, who already possesses everything and has no desire to receive? What good to Him, then, is a blessing from us? To find the answer, let us turn once again to the humble apple.

Nothing in the orchard is more artistically constructed than the apple (which, incidentally, is not specified as the forbidden fruit of Eden). Certainly, as do all gifts from God, the perfectly constructed apple bears a spiritual energy. But it also contains a problem. Because the otherwise innocent apple is a physical manifestation of the world of the Opponent, it imprisons the energy that must be free if it is to benefit us as the Creator intends. Remember, Malchut, the world of physical illusion in which we live, contains that one percent of darkness extant in a universe otherwise flooded with the Light. Since we who dwell in this dark corner have been endowed by the Creator with free will, the Light can penetrate only where we grant it permission through acts of positivity and sharing. Eat the apple without thought and the spiritual energy it contains will remain locked in the darkness of physicality. As a result, it will deliver little beyond a calorie or two of nutrition, quickly used up and forgotten.

To free energy from its mundane jail of physicality, one must bless the Lord, even as one consumes the gift. The blessing consists of specific Hebrew phrases, which need only be scanned with the eye if one is not literate in Hebrew. The full compendium of these phrases is contained in the English-Hebrew prayer book of The Kabbalah Centre.

While these phrases are important, they are not the only source from which the blessing can be drawn. Every positive, unselfish, sharing act we commit blesses the Lord because it releases the imprisoned energy inherent in whatever act is performed. In the case of the apple—or the various viands that make up the average person's dinner these days—the uttered prayer may serve as a vehicle of blessing, but, as discussed in the last chapter, it must be delivered with the kavanah of specific intent. It must be focused with laser intensity upon the apple or the meal, and it must be uttered with an open heart and a conscious desire to share. As a matter of restriction, it helps if one consciously leaves ten percent of the apple or the meal uneaten. Even if that 10 percent is "wasted," the intent to leave something for someone else vindicates the waste and blesses the Lord by setting free spiritual Light.

Bless and Receive

A passage in the Talmud observes that "more than the calf wants to suckle, the cow wants to nurse." In short, in metaphysical terms, the Creator wants to impart beneficence even more than we, His creations, want to receive it. But without our blessing, which is to say, our permission, He is unable to share with us His great gifts of continuity, order, and certainty. Since desire to share is His only desire, to deny Him, by means of our free will, the opportunity to share is to rob Him of that which rightfully is His. When we rob a bank, we risk the loss of freedom; when we rob the Lord, we risk losing everything that makes life worth living.

Which, of course, brings us back to the bank and the account we would like to be able to set up against negative times to come.

Spiritual energy exists outside of what we perceive as time, space, and motion. It is responsible for all healing, eternal life, wisdom, beauty, and joy in this world. Only by means of the blessing can we access these things. The metaphysical process by which this is done is abstruse, but Rabbi Ashlag, a 20th century visionary and Kabbalist, explains its essence this way.

All the good work we perform in this world is subject to entropy. We may quickly forget the good feeling we receive by helping someone else, and they in turn may forget the essence of the gift. The positive energy gained thus fades away. As a result, when the Opponent once again presents us with a bill of negativity, ranging from a bad mood to a major tragedy, we have no funds with which to pay it. But, according to the great Kabbalist Rabbi Ashlag, a blessing of the Lord always results in the receipt of a portion of positivity, which then is elevated to a level of dematerialization. In the metaphysical terminology with which this chapter is concerned, the differentiated tree thus is rolled back to the undifferentiated seed, which then is translated all the way up the circuitry of the Tree of Life to the Sfira Binah, where it receives a spiritual permanence before it is transported back to our world of existence. In short, whether born of eating an apple with gratitude, reveling in a breathtaking sunset, creating a work of art, making love, or just plain being thoroughly decent to a fellow human being, the portion of positivity we receive is no longer subject to entropy and becomes money in the bank.

But there is more to achieving this state of affairs than merely wishing it were so. Another piece of cosmic software must be called on line. It is called the Ana Beko'ach—by any measure the most powerful prayer, or, more properly, verbal construct ever devised. Come now, and taste of its power.

CHAPTER 5

THE ANA BEKO'ACH

In the beginning, the Lord created heaven and earth. And the earth was without form, and void.

—Genesis 1:1, 2.

The Language of Creation

Back in 1968, the crew of Apollo 8—the first manned spacecraft ever actually to reach the moon—mesmerized television audiences all over the world by reciting the opening lines of the Bible as their capsule skimmed over the lunar surface with cameras rolling.

Astronauts Frank Borman, James Lovell, and William Anders almost certainly never knew it, but the power of those first words, had they been rendered in Hebrew, would have far exceeded that of the mighty Saturn V rocket that had propelled them into the vastness of space. The words in Hebrew, phonetically rendered, are these:

Ana - beko'ach - G'dulat - Y'mincha - Tatir - T'zrurah
Kabel - Rinat - Amchah - Sagvenu - Tahareinu - Nora
Na - Gibor - Dorshei - Yechudecha - K'evavat - Shamrem
Barchem - Taharem - Rachamei - Tzidkatcha - Tamid - Gamlem
Chasin - Kadosh - B'rov - Tuvcha - Nahel - Adatecha

Yachid - Ge'eh - L'amcha - P'neh - Zochrei - K'dushatecha
Shav'atenu - Kabel - Ushma - Tza'akateinu - Yode'a - Ta'alumot

This is the language of Creation itself and, consequently, of rebirth, regeneration, and even immortality.

Once again, the esoteric science of Kabbalistic numerology plays a vital role, the essence of which will be spelled out here for those with a mathematical inclination. Use of the Ana beko'ach does not require mastery of the math, but even for the novice, the numbers do reveal the exquisite balance and symmetry of the prayer's construction.

The Ana beko'ach contains 42 words that, in Kabbalistic numerology, correspond directly to the 42 Hebrew letters of the Creative process. The Ana beko'ach is divided into seven lines, which can be seen as DNA sequences since they represent origins of seven different types of energy, each stemming from one of seven Sfirot in the Tree of Life, from Chesed all the way down to Malchut. Each line, or sequence, contains six words. Six times seven equals 42, which again corresponds directly to the number of first letters of each words in the prayer.

Each word contains two parts—a single first letter that serves as the seed of what the full word will be when made manifest, even as an apple seed contains root, trunk, and branch of the tree to come. And there are times when first letters of all the words in a phrase form a seed word that encompasses everything the phrase has to say.

In any case, when the Ana beko'ach is said—upon awakening every morning and again every evening at sunset—one should consciously visualize the first letter of every word pronounced.

Then there is virtually no positive need or desire that the prayer cannot address.

The Ana beko'ach can be used to protect the practitioner and his or her loved ones from evil, to sustain them in time of need, to heal them in illness, and to comfort them in grief. In short, practitioners have the power, by way of the Ana beko'ach, to secure anything that rightly and justly is theirs. No one can use it to rob a bank or harm a perceived enemy, but no true Kabbalist would even attempt such a negative use of a holy prayer.

The Ana beko'ach

(Read from right to left)

צב עב Capricorn Aquarius	צרורה t'zrurah	תתיר tatir	ימינך y'mincha	גדולת g'dulat	בכח beko'ach	אנא ana	חסד Chesed **1**
קג סג Sagittarius Pisces	נורא nora	טהרנו tahareinu	שגבנו sagvenu	עמך amchah	רנת rinat	קבל kabel	גבורה Gvurah **2**
דן דה Aries Scorpio	שמרם shamrem	כבבת k'evavat	יחודך yechudecha	דורשי dorshei	גבור gibor	נא na	תפארת Tiferet **3**
כט Leo	גמלם gamlem	תמיד tamid	צדקתך tzidkatcha	רחמי rachamei	טהרם taharem	ברכם barchem	נצח Netzach **4**
פל פו Taurus Libra	עדתך adatecha	נהל nahel	טובך tuvcha	ברוב b'rov	קדוש kadosh	חסין chasin	הוד Hod **5**
רי רז Gemini Virgo	קדושתך k'dushatecha	זוכרי zochrei	פנה p'neh	לעמך l'amcha	גאה ge'eh	יחיד yachid	יסוד Yesod **6**
חת Cancer	תעלומות ta'alumot	יודע yode'a	צעקתנו tza'akateinu	שמע ushma	קבל kabel	שועתנו shav'atenu	מלכות Malchut **7**

said silently

ברוך שם כבוד מלכותו לעולם ועד
va'ed l'olam malchutoh kevod shem baruch

73

To channel the power of spiritual Light to any particular goal or problem, one must say the prayer in full while concentrating specifically on the line representing the energy type needed to address the subject in question. In general, the lines, with their Sfirotic connections and practical applications, are these:

Line 1: Chesed—The most powerful line of the prayer, to be concentrated upon in time of extreme stress or danger; the DNA sequence of the power to provide sustenance in time of need

Line 2: Gvurah—The power to move events and control negative external forces

Line 3: Tiferet—The ability to make the right decision, with the proper balance and compassion

Line 4: Netzach—The endurance necessary to follow through and prove victorious

Line 5: Hod—Deep insight, almost clairvoyance

Line 6: Yesod—The ability to find peace and inner quiet

Line 7 : Malchut—Renewal, for starting again

Taking Control

In this age, the plague of petty bureaucracy is familiar to almost everyone. Overly complicated paperwork and small-minded, impractical rules can frustrate our plans and bog down our lives in everything from securing a bank loan or motivating a contractor to securing any one of a hundred permits necessary these days to live, work, or do business. Putting a stop to official foot-dragging does not exactly fall into the categories of resurrection or the saving of lives, but the Ana beko'ach is a tool for all uses and, by way of example, it can even be used to beat the bureaucracy.

In this case, as the practitioner recites the prayer, he or she must concentrate the kavanah, or direction, of the prayer on the second line of the Ana beko'ach, which is ruled by Gvurah. Gvurah is the Sfira of restriction, discipline, and judgment, and under its stern influence, those bureaucrats will act with compassion and reason if you bring its power to bear upon them. They won't know why, but they will be unable to resist the influence and your problem will become their top priority.

The Ana beko'ach is structured in such a fashion that it can bring harm to no one. There is a bit of folk wisdom that says, "Be careful what you wish for; you might get it," but the implied danger does not apply here. As a pure conveyance of spiritual Light, the Ana beko'ach is fail-safe. When you recite it, you connect with the celestial bodies that are the vehicles, or catalysts, by which particular energies are transferred from the Tree of Knowledge to the Tree of Life.

The prayer always is followed by what might be called a grounding line: Baruch, Shem, Kevod, Malkhuto, Le'Olam, Va'ed. These words are said silently after the full prayer is recited to make the Holy Name manifest in our world of Malchut. In short, after we have done the meditation and prayed, we must connect the prayer, bringing it from the metaphysical realm to the physicality of whatever we're praying for or meditating upon.

And a Little Child Shall Lead Them

Children display the essence of the Light of the Creator without even trying. We know instinctively not to tread on all of the miracles and the million magical possibilities a little child may believe in, thought foolish by most adults. As we mature, something happens to our beliefs. We become adults and, hence, adulterated, and with that adulteration comes the onset of doubt.

Suddenly, we are too intelligent, too educated, too experienced in the ways of the world to believe in fairy tales, miracles, or the possibility of physical regeneration or metaphysical healing. Our egos tell us even to be proud of our disbelief. As a result, when it comes to tapping the full power of the Light, we don't even try.

It cannot be said too often: doubt is the Opponent's deadliest weapon; doubt turns off the lights. And ego is just another name for the Opponent. Fortunately for us, scientific events are storming the barricades of some of this doubt, making believers of even the most skeptical.

By way of example, let us consider a TV news anchorman sitting in his network's New York studio while he appears in millions of homes all over the world at the same time. A scant half-century ago, the very idea would have been so deeply embedded in metaphysics as to be beyond the imagination of anyone outside the scientific or supernatural community. How in the world would the process whereby Dan Rather is transmitted have been explained to us before we actually saw a television set? Today, nobody gives the phenomenon a second thought. Science has caught up with Kabbalah, and the only amazing thing about the fact that Rather rides orbiting satellite transponders is the fact that no one gives it a thought. Why doesn't the average person stop to ask, "What really is happening here?"

Kabbalah explains the multi-location phenomenon this way. The actual newsman is not the one seen in the flesh by his wife, his son, his daughter, and the host of colleagues. The real anchorman is the 99 percent of the man who is not seen by anyone. The physical person—the one actually sitting at the anchor desk—is an illusion, just as everything in the physical world is illusory. But in developing global television, physical science has wrought the first step in a truly metaphysical "miracle." The scientists themselves have not yet grasped the magnitude of what they have done. Through the magic of camera, transponder, and satellite dish, they have managed to dematerialize the physical man, beginning to free his inherent spiritual Light. Only thus could a person sitting in front of a TV camera be in millions of places at the same time.

Of course the image of the man on the television screen, projected there by a physical transponder on a satellite high above the earth's atmosphere, is not "pure" in terms of spiritual energy. A fraction of the man's physicality rides piggyback. Since this hitchhiker is physical, the real image cannot be imbued with the newsman's individual consciousness. But nonetheless, something truly miraculous happens every day as we receive these broadcast transmissions.

Children, in a sense, know this better than their parents. They feel the reality of these images more strongly than their overly rational elders. These elders, had they been born a century earlier, would have scoffed at the idea of TV, just as many of them would scoff at the power of the Ana beko'ach.

When Science Fiction Becomes Science

In Ray Bradbury's classic science fiction tale, *Fahrenheit 451*, a bored housewife, living in a world where books are forbidden and television is mandatory, is able not only to watch her favorite soap operas but to take a role in them as well, interacting on an individual basis with the cast of actors. And while she performs this interaction, millions of other equally bored housewives are doing the same thing. Actors in the cast have no problem carrying on simultaneous dialogue with all of them. Believe it or not, the story now is closer to reality than you can imagine.

As the collective consciousness of humankind rises to that metaphysical plateau from which most of us can perceive the reality of the Tree of Life, any human being will instantly have the capacity to come into a million homes, not only to talk to us, but to discuss events with us and field our questions as well. And this is a phenomenon that will be made possible by the next generation of transponders—one called the Ana beko'ach.

Under terms of this metaphysical transformation, when a person's image is cloned back to Malchut via television, it is free to spread unchecked by the limitations of time, space, and motion. In the same light, any time we use the Ana beko'ach to connect with the living letters of the Aleph Bet and dematerialize physicality, we release the power of spiritual Light, making all things possible.

Remember, in the beginning, our conflicted souls rejected the Light of the Creator on the grounds that we could not accept that which we had not earned, thus creating Bread of Shame with its concealing prison of physicality. The Creator then bowed to our wishes and restricted the spiritual Light. Spiritual Light now comes in packets of physical energy, giving us an opportunity to release it. We do this by removing Bread of Shame in the same way in which God created it—with restriction, which is the intent and the act of sharing. Then, in a marvelous act of co-creation, we earn the right, as co-creators, not only to receive all that the Creator wishes to give us, but to re-create ourselves as well. This will become possible when we have removed the cause that forced Him to restrict in the first place. And when we have learned to use Ana beko'ach.

A Matter of Matter

The average person would say that a table utterly destroyed by fire has disappeared, but that would not be an accurate assessment. The interior space once occupied by the table does not disappear. Its atomic structure continues beyond the life of what we perceive as wood; it is just that atoms in that structure no longer behave as a cohesive body. And therein lies a paradox.

Atoms freely drifting about in interstellar space have no power. In the physical universe, they present nothing more than an undifferentiated potential—the seeds of what we perceive as reality. But when they become differentiated through being confined as molecules forming the structure of the table, they express the power of solidity. A table is a useful thing to have, but with the spiritual energy imprisoned within the table's physical structure, that table also radiates a massive amount of chaos. Bang your knee against the table's leg or slam your fist on its surface and you are likely to accrue a nasty bruise. Try to run across the room and the table is in the way. We naturally want to utilize the table's useful aspect, while nullifying the chaos or inconvenience it can cause. In short, the goal is to be able to dine at the table or use its surface as the physical prop necessary to write a letter, then rise and simply walk through it when we are finished.

Think of the consequences of chaos removed from our lives. A reactive person incensed at something the news anchor has said on the evening news might, in momentary rage, hurl a brick through the television screen right into the broadcaster's face. The news anchor, of course, will not feel the brick because the image on that screen is a manifestation of spiritual energy, and so no physical assault can touch the anchor materially. Accomplish the power of dematerialization and the same principle can apply to any person, in the flesh—a phenomenon that will thwart all the muggers and maniacs and drive-by shooters who wish to cause us harm.

Spot a truck careening down a hill with its brakes gone and headed for a crowd of people in an intersection. In an instant, that truck can be converted to nothing more than a shadow that passes through the crowd, leaving everyone unharmed—before it then proceeds to its destination and delivers its cargo as though nothing out of the ordinary had happened.

Impossible? Not at all. When fire has reduced the table to ashes, it no longer has the power to support utensils, and a human hand can pass through it with ease. The goal of Kabbalah is to manage the dematerialization of matter wherever it presents an aspect of chaos, pain, or inconvenience in our lives, without losing the positive aspect of the object in question. Whenever the dematerialization process is accomplished, the Light of the Creator is allowed to dominate the object and no chaotic consequences can emerge from it.

We accomplish this, once again, by means of the power of the Ana beko'ach brought to bear upon the aspect of restriction. The molecules locking the spiritual energy into the solidity of the table are there for a reason. The reason is this: In the beginning, the Creator had to invoke restriction to create the physical universe and give us a chance to remove our Bread of Shame by restricting our own desire to receive for the self alone. If we can accomplish this, if we can restrict our own desire to receive for the self alone, nothing is beyond us.

Breaking the Barriers

Apollo 8's first moon flight did more than merely entrance a worldwide television audience. For the first time, that tiny spacecraft, with its three-man crew, brought things metaphysical in terms easily understood by the public into the physical world. Apollo 8 broke the barrier once and for all between the physical and the metaphysical by carrying its cargo beyond the gravitational grip of Earth and into the gravity field of another world.

Astronauts who followed them in subsequent space missions routinely started "going EVA" (extra-vehicular activity), as NASA bureaucrats call the now common space walk undertaken when a crewmember steps outside the spaceship to move in the hard vacuum of space. At that point, a mortal man or woman, tethered to an orbiting spacecraft, literally could stroll around the world in roughly an hour's time. Out there, beyond the stifling grip of gravity and the ever-present rasp of friction, the desire to receive for the self alone is diminished in yet another wedding of the physical and metaphysical sciences.

Time, space, and motion do not exist in the Tree of Life reality, and for the first time, with their orbital diminution visible in space flight, the concept suddenly becomes clear. With that, the Kabbalistic claim that great saints and sages of the past literally could fly to anyplace in the universe no longer seems quite so bizarre.

But something even more important happened in the years following the breakthrough called Apollo 8. For the first time in history, the universe truly opened up to humankind, making the influence of Kabbalistic astrology, which is an integral part of the Ana beko'ach, a point of comprehensible logic. Planetary influences are precisely what the prayer is designed to control. But before we explore those cosmic particulars, let us examine further its structure and meaning.

As the coded biblical explanation of the Ana beko'ach, the Zohar cites Isaiah 63:4, which says, "For the day of vengeance is in my heart." Always remember, the Bible is a code, and its tales are not always to be taken literally. In this case, "vengeance" means "dominion," and the phrase "in my heart" actually is the code of the Sfira Binah, which also is called "heart." Binah also might be called "the energy store," since it is to Binah, at the top of the left-hand column in the Tree of Life, that the Kabbalist goes to tap the power of the Light. By means of the Ana beko'ach through the influence of Binah, one is able to take dominion in one's life away from the Opponent, just as the Israelites were able to take dominion away from the Egyptians and be freed from bondage. To complete the cycle, the numerical value of the Hebrew phrase "in my heart" is 42—again, the same as that of the Ana beko'ach.

The Universal Tool

There are no problems in life for which the Ana beko'ach cannot successfully be used as a solution. Its practice can create miracles, control events, and cure illnesses. So far, there is no known scientific reason why it should work, nor is there any scientific data that it does work—but it does. As the very language of Creation, the prayer—or construct, as it might better be called—has been around since before the Big Bang. The patriarch Abraham knew and used the Ana beko'ach, as did his descendants, but unfortunately, like Kabbalah itself, the means of explaining it were not available until the advent of quantum physics and other more recent breakthroughs in the physical and medical sciences. The Ana beko'ach therefore languished in dark corners of Talmudic discourse, unknown and unavailable to a world that has always desperately needed it.

To utilize the power of the Ana beko'ach, one first must be in a state of restriction, which, in this case, is the concentration of kavanah. The other requirement is a state of sharing, which is to say, the keeping of an open heart. These two most vital elements have been deemed from the dawn of Creation to be the ones by which Bread of Shame can be removed from our lives, giving us the ability to accept the full beneficence of the Lord.

If these conditions are not met, then the practitioners, however involuntarily, pass up what the Light is so eager to offer. At that point, the transgressors have, in fact, created their own adversary, setting up obstacles that will prevent the Light from coming to their assistance. The Light, after all, must follow the requirements of Creation, the chief of which states that "there is no coercion in abundance and spirituality." Neither gifts nor elevation of the soul can be forced upon a recipient. Approach the Light with any attitude but a desire to receive for the sake of sharing, and the whole exercise becomes food for the Opponent. Remember, the Opponent is the one who collects every bit of the energy we reject through the desire to receive for the self alone. Stolen Light is his life's blood.

But approach the Ana beko'ach in the proper light, and the Opponent is evicted for good. Here is how it works:

The practitioner must say the prayer, meditatively and in full, every day upon awakening in the morning and again at sunset. In the course of recitation, kavanah, or specific direction, must be given to the line marking the current month—information available in the chart on page 73. By this means, the Kabbalist is able to cleanse the month of any negativity that might accrue to it and hence avoid negative consequences in his or her own life for the course of that month.

The Only Astrologer You'll Ever Need Is You

In conventional astrology, while the stars and planets do not compel, they do impel, affecting people and events in a variety of ways frequently beyond their control. But the practitioner of Kabbalistic astrology has an advantage. By using the Ana beko'ach, Kabbalists actually are able to impose their own will upon the planets. Planets, like people who exist in the duality of a body and a soul, have both a physical and a metaphysical aspect, and because the Opponent lurks in the dark corners of physicality looking for a chance to work his mischief, one must rule the planets if one hopes to profit by their emanations. The Opponent has no real power of his own, but because of the physical existence of planets in the zodiac, he can hitch a ride on any of their emanations. By using the Ana beko'ach, the Kabbalist is able to address Mars or Venus or Mercury and command it to transmit only its positive energy, leaving negativity behind, for the monthly ruling planet.

All the influences present in our world reach us by astrological transmissions, and most people are forced to take the bad right along with the good. Only the Kabbalist, with the Ana beko'ach, can keep the Opponent out of the mix by restricting the negative energies of the planet. But remember, just because the month has been cleansed does not mean your or anyone else's thinking has been purified. If your boss is after your job, your bank has erroneously closed out your account, or your "significant other" prefers someone else, a cleansed month will help, but more is needed.

Of the seven lines that constitute the Ana beko'ach, the first, ruled by the Sfira of Chesed and containing the cosmic DNA of the planet Saturn, is the most powerful. And why Saturn, rather than Mars, Jupiter, or Pluto? The answer was spelled out more than 1,000 years ago by Italian Kabbalist, physician, and astronomer Shabattai Donolo. Donolo worked out the blueprint of Creation centuries before the discovery of DNA, which really is the only means by which such things can be explained to the layperson today.

Donolo held that Saturn was established with a flawless metaphysical DNA dominated by the Hebrew letter Bet, the single instrument with which God created the universe. The seven Hebrew letters contained in the rest of the sequence participated collectively in the creation of all seven planets. But the letter Bet was the prime mover in the celestial formula containing the all-inclusive sequence.

The metaphysical DNA of Hebrew letters also determined every tiny detail of the planets and of all living organisms, and, with Saturn, emerged as day one of the biblical story of Creation. Each day of the week has its own specific energy, represented by characteristics of the seven lower Sfirot on the Tree of Life: Chesed for Sunday, Gvurah for Monday, Tiferet for Tuesday, Netzach for Wednesday, Hod for Thursday, Yesod for Friday, and Malchut for Saturday. The seven days are further broken down into the seven lines of the Ana beko'ach, as explained by the chart on page 74, which spells out the application of each line when the prayer is recited. Day one of the biblical Creation story, the first verse of which is the Ana beko'ach and known to us as Sunday, combines all of the seven intelligent energy forms into one unified whole.

There is much, much more to the intricate mechanics of Creation, with each subsequent day producing its own planet and planetary attributes. A full dissertation on the subject would fill a complete book, and the sample offered here is designed merely to show that the Ana beko'ach, which contains it all, is the most powerful tool available today for infusion of the Tree of Life DNA sequence into our lives. It exists as a link with the hidden powers of our subconscious. We do not have to acquire these powers; we already possess them. Within the inner recesses of our consciousness lies everything that is necessary to enhance our physical and mental well-being. Once we have achieved control of all our thoughts, which primarily is what the Ana beko'ach empowers us to do, body consciousness will no longer interfere.

Certainty Is the Antithesis of Chaos

Centuries ago, the prophet Isaiah peered far into the future. Of what he saw, he wrote: "Then the eyes of the blind shall be opened and the ears of the deaf shall be unstopped. Then shall the lame man leap as an animal and the tongue of the dumb shall sing" (35:5–6).

Another prophet, Jeremiah, followed that up with a vision of his own when he wrote, "There will no longer be the necessity for one to request of his neighbor, teach me wisdom, as it is written, one day they will no longer teach every man his neighbor and every man his brother, saying, Know the Lord, for they shall all know Me, from the youngest to the oldest of them" (31:34).

Our age also is known as the age of the information superhighway—an age characterized by an explosion of knowledge at every cultural and economic level and by advances in medicine and physics that border on the miraculous. Who can doubt that the time spoken of by Isaiah and Jeremiah finally is here?

CHAPTER 6

SCIENCE AND SPIRIT

Physics, as we know it, will be over in six months.

—British physicist Max Born, 1882–1970

Through the Looking Glass

This pronouncement by Max Born, made in the late 1920s when the new science of quantum mechanics made its debut on the stage of academia, carried both a ring of triumph and a grace note of despair. Things under the rule of theoretical physics had been so tidy and secure; now, as the atom crumbled into smaller pieces, and the pieces crumbled into smaller pieces still, all previous assumptions of surety were being swept away.

At the subatomic level, which Born himself had helped discover and define, reality can't even be observed or measured with accuracy. Under the new science's inherent uncertainty principle, the very act of observing a particle changes its location and behavior. And, if that particle happens to be a bit of matter called a photon, it can become a wave of energy, then revert to matter again as though it were a prop in a magician's sleight-of-hand stage show.

Suddenly, with the advent of quantum physics, the universe was being seen through Alice's looking glass, in which nothing stands still and things no longer are what they seem to be.

Although physicists were starting to realize the old order was over, many, including even the great Albert Einstein, never quite made peace with the new one. Had a Kabbalist worked in their midst, they might have found the enlightenment needed to understand the importance of their own discoveries.

The Kabbalist is accustomed to the interchangeability of matter and energy, and to subatomic activity that carries its own unique degree of intelligence, defying the constraints of time, space, and motion.

Geniuses of Yin and Yang

The great Renaissance artists, Leonardo da Vinci and Michelangelo, sharply disagreed on the quality of light. Da Vinci contended that all was darkness, and that for the sake of contrast, the artist had to force light into being when he painted a picture. Michelangelo insisted that the opposite was true: the universe consisted of light, and in order to create a picture, the artist was forced to inject it with darkness.

Before the Big Bang, in Ain Soph where our souls were created, there was nothing in the universe but Light: the all-pervading ambient Light of Creation. That universe of Light is what Kabbalah helps us regain, and what Michelangelo believed in. Michelangelo knew, however, that darkness was required to make a painting, to make things appear in this reality ruled by the Tree of Knowledge. And since most people's perception of reality is 99 percent darkness and one percent light, perhaps da Vinci was right as well. His transcendent paintings, drawings, and inventions brought more light into the world than thousands of other artists combined.

Scientists have been studying light for centuries, and they have come to many conclusions, some true, some erroneous. In the 18th century they determined that it travels at a constant speed. Then, in 1887, Edward Morley and Albert Michelson, both Nobel laureates in physics, conducted a light-speed experiment at the Case School of Applied Science in Cleveland. They found that the speed of light was always the same, no matter if the source or the observer was in motion or at rest. This set up the seemingly absurd proposition that a measurement of light speed taken by someone moving toward a light source would be identical with that taken by one moving away from it. Einstein later came up with the math nailing down the absolute universal speed limit of 186,000 miles per second—no warp drive, and hence no interstellar sojourning for us except in our imagination or on Star Trek. Subsequent findings have indicated that light can be measured either as a stream of particles called photons, or as a wave of energy.

But, for all their study, the scientists still have not managed to unscramble the mystery of illumination, which, in the Kabbalistic view, is simply this: Light is, in fact, motionless; there is no movement and therefore no "speed of light." The Zohar teaches that at the time of Creation, Light was designed to shine from the beginning to the end of the universe's existence. But when the Lord, for whom all time is like a vast mural, devoid of the linear illusion of past, present, and future, reflected upon the truly evil people who were destined to appear in this material realm, He decided to deny them use of the Light. As it is put in the Book of Job, "He withheld from the wicked their Light." At that point, He pledged to make the Light "available to the righteous in the world to come." The standard religious interpretation of such a promise would imply that "the world to come" is the one set aside for righteous souls after death—heaven, if you will—but that is not what the Zohar teaches at all. The world to come is nothing more than the one the Kabbalist strives to enter in this life, in the here and now, the here and now that is also eternity.

The argument between physics and metaphysics about the nature of light is not a trivial one. Einstein spent his life searching for a grand unified theory that would explain everything. He never found it, but the Kabbalist has operated under a grand unified theory from the beginning. It is that the spiritual Light overrides all limitations, including the rational mind's notion that yesterday, today, and tomorrow are distinct frames of time that must forever remain separate from one another. Under such a paradigm, it is impossible to peer either into the future or go back into the past, and the only thing holding that paradigm together is the erroneous concept of a light-speed barrier. In truth, the Light has quantum qualities capable of rolling yesterday, today, and tomorrow into the here and now, devoid of the uncertainty and fragmentation of time as we perceive it. The Light embraces and erases the concepts of time, space, and motion.

Just Throw the Switch

Picture yourself in a movie theater after the show, when the moviegoers all are set to leave. But instead of the lights coming up, all go out, plunging the auditorium into utter darkness. Suddenly, uncertainty sets in as to where the exits are, where the seats are located, and where the aisles may be found. Chaos rules and panic rises. But the growing bedlam subsides the instant the house lights are switched back on. Order and a feeling of well-being immediately are restored. Simple as it may sound, that is exactly what happens in the metaphysical realm as well, which is why the Opponent is the master of chaos and is eager to keep us all in the dark.

The Zohar is very clear about the grand unifying aspect of the spiritual Light, and its explanation takes us back to the meditation involving lights within lights among the Sfirot. There are, we are taught, not one, but two Lights of primary concern in our day-to-day lives. One is the concealed Light, which does not shine and is not detectable by the world at large but which can be used by the righteous at any time of need. And by "righteous," we mean anyone who, through Kabbalistic application, has managed to remove Bread of Shame from his or her life. The second Light, known by its code name Tov, or "good," is drawn from the concealed Light and shines for all the world. Its coded source is found in Genesis: "And the Lord saw the Light, and it was good." This is the Light that sustains and maintains the physical universe.

Finally, the Creator added, "To you who fear my name, the sun of righteousness shall arise with healing in its wings." What emerges from all of this, of course, is a grand unified force available to all who can connect with the concealed Light. Not only is this Light capable of freeing the human mind from the limited concept of fragmented time as expressed in terms of past, present, and future, but it also enables those making the connection to enjoy the benefits of its quantum healing power.

But quantum healing of all disease, which will be dealt with in detail in the next chapter, lies within the concealed Light where the highways of interconnectedness produce instantaneous information. The delicate web of intelligence that binds the body together permits a platelet to rush to the site of a wound.

It travels there for the express purpose of forming a clot, and when it arrives, it knows exactly where to go and what to do. Human-made drugs lack the natural intelligence of bodily functions and chemicals and are therefore not as effective as the inherent healing powers we carry within our physical selves.

E Pluribus Unum

If there now exists a courtship between physics and metaphysics, the two still are not quite ready for matrimony. They have, after all, been feuding for the approximately 300 years of modern science's sway. Science, some might say, still has a long way to go.

But the physical sciences finally are beginning to catch up with knowledge held for centuries in Kabbalah. The quantum theory, which made its grand entrance in 1925, overthrew long-cherished notions about our universe. It destroyed the fundamental axiom that what could not be observed or measured in the laboratory simply could not exist. One of the first casualties of the quantum revolution was Einstein and his school of relativity. Einstein never could accept the uncertainty inherent in the quantum theory. It meant that the five senses and the laboratory no longer could predict with absolute accuracy the motion of things in the universe.

Quantum theory overturns our belief, based in the Tree of Knowledge reality, that common sense serves as the best guide to the world around us. We now know that our rational consciousness belongs to the world of confusion described by the formulation of quantum mechanics. As a result, scientists and laypeople alike have been forced to elevate their consciousness above the level of commonsense thinking and accept a new meaning to Shakespeare's observation, in Hamlet: "There are more things in heaven and earth, Horatio, than are dreamt of in your philosophy."

What is most surprising is that science can observe the orderliness of nature, yet fail to ascribe to it a higher intelligence than anything humankind can conceive or maintain. This natural intelligence pervades everything in the universe; it is a quantum network that affects at once the billions of cells in our bodies, the movement of financial markets and global politics, and the workings of galaxies. This vast database of information is available to all of us, but without access to the concealed Light, we cannot see it, let alone utilize it.

Although our limited rational mind perceives people and things as separate entities, each possessing its own local, independent reality, the Zohar and the latest science sees connections between everything. The famous Irish physicist John Bell formulated the *Bell Theorem*, which maintains that all things and events within the universe are interconnected. British physicist David Bohm, working with Bell's theory, concluded that an invisible field holds all of reality together and that there is an intimate interconnection of different systems that are not in spatial contact.

This is precisely what the Zohar implies with respect to the concealed Light. The second Light—the visible Tov, which is drawn from it—does not give a complete description of the whole of reality. Like all things in the Tree of Knowledge, Tov, the drawn Light, is a force for both good and evil. The drawn Light maintains the stability of the universe by, among other things, keeping the planets from crashing into each other like so many cosmic bumper cars, but it still contains an element of chaos. Only in the concealed Light do probabilities and uncertainties cease to exist. Physicists express this idea in what they call a sub-quantum theory. They feel if they could only come to grips with the additional information that would be provided by this sub-quantum theory, they could predict the outcome of all cosmic events. That sub-quantum existence, in the form of the concealed Light, is at the fingertips of the Kabbalist.

From "Seeing Is Believing" to "Believing Is Seeing"

In 1927, another physicist bowed without knowing it to the wisdom of Kabbalah. Niels Bohr ended the classical idea of objectivity by proclaiming that the physical world is an illusion. "The real world," he said, "lies one step beyond, where a chair is not a chair until we observe it and proclaim it so." "That chair does not exist," he said, "until we acknowledge its existence." Overnight, the common expression, "If I hadn't seen it, I never would have believed it," became the inverse: "If I hadn't believed it, I never would have seen it."

But even for Bohr and the scientific colleagues of his day, a cloud of common sense obscured the horizons they were trying to see. Witness this reported conversation between Einstein and one of his students:

Einstein (in the classroom): Nothing exists out there unless we determine its existence.

Student: Does that mean if someone has a cancerous tumor, all he has to do is think that it is not there and it will go away?

Einstein: In theory, that is absolutely correct.

Student: Then why doesn't the medical establishment accept these teachings of the scientific community and put an end to the disease of cancer?

Einstein: While in theory it is correct, their consciousness cannot come to grips with it on the level of physical reality. Most of medical science rejects such thinking outright.

The class ends and the student accompanies Einstein back to his home on campus. When they arrive, Einstein, who is notoriously absentminded, finds the door locked and belatedly remembers he left the key inside. He cannot open the door.

Student: What's the problem? Why don't we go inside?

Einstein (rather sheepishly): I left the key inside.

Student (remembering the lecture): Why not consciously consider the door as not being there, and simply walk right in?

Einstein can only shrug. His rational mind would not allow him to put his own quite profound understanding into practice.

Einstein was not alone, of course. Many people, out of stubbornness and pride, perhaps, will not permit themselves to leave the rational consciousness of confusion, chaos, and uncertainty behind. For them, the price will be a permanent cyclical future of good and evil, ups and downs, brief triumphs and dark tragedies. For scientist and layperson alike, this age demands revolutionary thinking, and it must begin by abandonment of the Opponent and everything he stands for, including our own egos.

The Opponent loves ego; ego is his favorite henchman. Our egos go instantly to red alert when threatened. The ego insists that when we disregard it, we lose our identity, our sense of self. Put another way, the ego is the vital force behind rational consciousness.

The rational mind is subject to every whim of the ego. Our perception of reality depends completely upon how that perception accommodates the individual ego. That is why several people may view the same object or event, then give conflicting, even diametrically opposite reports as to what they saw. Our egos tie results to fragmentation, which then fosters the uncertainty that inevitably leads to chaos.

Metaphysical Networks

To clarify the point, consider the television traffic reporter covering rush hour in a big city from the vantage point of a helicopter. She can see the traffic flow far better than drivers on the ground; her perch affords her a dimension that condenses space and allows her to focus on all of the automobiles on the highway below simultaneously. The individual driver operates blindly, inasmuch as he cannot see the traffic very far in front, behind, or on either side of his automobile. The driver can make guesses based on his self-interest, and try another route. We all know what happens when the driver, with his limited perception, makes an incorrect call: hours of driving around; in short, chaos.

Only by tuning his radio to the helicopter report can the driver make a connection with the reporter, bring all the surrounding information into focus, and maybe avoid entrapment in grid-lock by taking an alternate route. The concealed Light is the helicopter; the radio is the Kabbalistic meditation that makes the connection. Anyone who has managed to change his or her essence to one of complete sharing can tune in to the quantum network.

To appreciate the awesome power of that network, let us now turn our attention to a Zoharic insight concerning the unifying implications of spatial dimension. The Book of Genesis tells the tale of a sojourning Jacob who elects to spend the night on a hillside of what then was a vast wilderness. As he sleeps, he dreams of a ladder reaching from Earth to Heaven, and at the top, the Lord appears to him to promise that he will be the father of a vast nation, and that he will rule over a holy temple, though it will not be built in his lifetime.

Jacob's resting place in the wilderness was far away from where the city of Jerusalem now stands. Yet that city—where not one but two temples eventually were to be built—and a vast nation yet to be born were rolled up and placed beneath his head that fateful night. In one moment of Jacob's vision, the entire nation of Israel and all of its institutions were formed in a seamless creation devoid of the restraints of time, space, or motion.

Prior to the coming of Einstein, when the Euclidean view of the world deemed that every aspect of existence occupied a separate compartment of reality, such a story was consigned to the dust-bin of mythology. Even now, the idea of such specific meta-physical networking is a hard pill for most physicists to swallow. But with the general theory of relativity suggesting that one interconnected underlying field exists for all transformations of space, time, mass, and energy, the concept at last has currency.

The idea of a universe in which all things are fused requires certain mental leaps, among them the understanding that sight, smell, taste, touch, and hearing all are rolled into one sense. Intuitively, we may already suspect that they are. How often, upon hearing something explained, have you concluded, "I see what you mean?" How often, upon seeing something suspicious, have you decided that "it just doesn't feel right" or that you "smell a rat"? Our senses are one with us.

The grand unified theory of the Light unites all the basic forces in creation and defines the universe as an all-embracing whole. Instead of separate, fragmented compartments, there is only one whole. Once we have broken free of the clutches of the lie of rational consciousness, a whole new, simple, beautiful world opens up for us.

Beyond the Senses

Kabbalists have known for millennia that the universe does more than resemble a great thought; the universe is a great thought. A basic tenet of Kabbalah is that knowledge is intelligence, which is to say it is a connection with the Tree of Life. Intelligence is energy, and the origin of all energy is the Light of the Creator. There is no room in this scenario for a mechanistic cosmos blindly ticking its way into eternity. The Creator is a thinker, not a tinker.

The universe, and humankind with it, is nothing more than an enormous composite of thought. The universe exists in our minds, our bodies, and everything we experience, touch, taste, see, and do. Illusory though they may be, every particle, antiparticle, neutron, and quark in the universe is directed by and acts according to the dictates of a particular intelligence.

There is a tale told of a legendary Kabbalist who, when invited for tea, asked his host for a cube of sugar. But he did not put the sugar in his tea, he simply looked at it, then sipped from his cup. Finding the tea too sweet, he broke the sugar cube in two and sipped again. He continued this process until the sweetness of the tea was to his liking.

The story illustrates how we can abandon our conventional understanding of the five senses by refusing to pass them through the screens established by our limited, fragmented, rational consciousness. Once we understand that the universe is not as fragmented as our senses suppose, we immediately experience beauty and wonderment.

The real problem—or opportunity—facing humankind today is the realization that space, once considered truly empty, is not empty at all. It is suffused with infinite and changeable fields of energy. Physicists cannot decide whether the total energy is negative or positive, but they do seem to agree that the totality of that energy is enormous. Inasmuch as energy is similar to mass, let us reflect for a moment on how this energy-filled "empty space" may exert its influence upon our thoughts.

Under the Kabbalistic tenet stating that as things are above, so they are below, most of the energy crackling in space is negative energy. We know that because we have put it there. Every negative act we commit goes into the great continuum that, under the rule of the Opponent, rains negativity back upon us. In truth, however, most of the 5 billion or so men and women now crowding planet Earth are not inherently evil, violent people. So why is there so much chaos?

Again, the answer is Murphy's law, which states, what can go wrong will go wrong. And it doesn't take much. The Opponent needs only one small negative break within the superhighway of energy to invade and contaminate the entire area. If our universe is part of a network of universes, connected by strings and submicroscopic tunnels of space and time, it is easy to see that a world of chaos might result from the smallest, apparently inconsequential rip in the fabric of the Light.

As a result, we live in a universe replete with chaotic systems. The inherent problem is this: no plan ever can be exactly linear because of the infinite number of energy intelligences that affect it, and even a well-thought-out plan—if there is such a thing—is subject to Murphy's Law. As a result, the Opponent can play with humankind as he chooses. He can get us coming and going, both through our negative thinking as well as through bad thinking that may seem on the surface benign, or even positive. The Opponent can get to us, for instance, through our complacency about our health. Most of us, as long as we are healthy, believe that our health will stay on course, despite statistics that say otherwise. Statistics and dire warnings always are taken to apply to others. The Opponent, who first guarantees that what can go wrong will go wrong, ironically has also brought us to the point where we begin to believe that nothing can go wrong where our lives are concerned. The only way for us to maintain our health, in fact, is by keeping a close connection with the Light of the Creator. As long as the highway is lit, the Opponent can occupy no part of it.

CHAPTER 7

SICKNESS AND HEALTH

If all the medicines known were thrown into the ocean, it would be the better for the human race and the worse for the fish.

—*Oliver Wendell Holmes, 1809–1894*

The "War" against Disease

The great 19th century Boston author, poet, and physician really didn't have a thing against the fish; it's just that he recognized within his own profession a central flaw that persists to this day. The vast majority of medicines, along with allopathic surgery and radiation techniques, treat the symptoms and ignore the causes of disease.

But first, let us make sure we are spelling the word right. It should be dis-ease, with a hyphen, because a loss of ease in the world of chaos is exactly what lies at the core of everything from chickenpox to cancer. Dis-ease, fostered by our own emotional outlooks and hidebound beliefs, literally means disruption of ease, a disturbance of the resting, motionless state of mind that leads to good health. It implies imbalance, lack of order, and the existence of chaotic conditions so omnipresent in our world.

We react to dis-ease with still another word that needs a hyphen to be fully understood. We become up-set, which is to say we experience a sensation of things not being set, and hence in disarray. We also can become distressed, depressed, dejected, and despondent, and all the terms have one common usage: they explain the symptom, not the problem.

Therein lies the fundamental barrier to finding solutions for the problems that plague us. We are unable or unwilling to probe further into primary causes, preferring the quick fix rather than any real mental or spiritual analysis. Even antibiotics, which were supposed to ring the death knell once and for all for infectious diseases, have been so overused as to be rendered virtually impotent. The Grolier Multimedia Encyclopedia (1993) concludes that 90 percent of all antibiotic prescriptions now issued are "unnecessary or inappropriate."

Modern medicine's allopathic approach tries to cure disease by producing a condition within the system either different from or opposite to the disease itself. If you have a fever, allopathic doctors say kill it with aspirin; if you have indigestion, they say reverse it with a spoonful or two of antacid. In short, in what might be described as the quantum of symptom disorders, they treat the superficial, outward symptoms of all illness, whether they be physical, mental, or sociological, while paying no attention whatsoever to the internal, metaphysical cause. Temporary relief thus becomes the prime goal in a corrupted perspective on the life sciences. A great deal of attention is paid to "winning the war" against disease, but the "war" seldom gives even lip service to prevention.

Still, even with a track record that might be regarded as dubious in any other field, allopathic medicine still holds sway, while healers using other approaches remain widely regarded as quacks and charlatans. Physicians alone, says conventional wisdom, have it in their power to heal bodies, but the truth is this: no physician ever healed anybody. When orthopedic surgeons set a broken arm or leg, do they actually do any healing? Of course not; the healing is a natural property of the body. The physician, who essentially acts as a mechanic or, if you will, an enabler, has no role in it. "Healers" of other disciplines also fall into this category.

Alternative Medicine

Alternative medicine has come to be closely aligned with the idea of healing. Homeopaths are treated now with scorn by the establishment, though they had many followers right after Samuel Hahnemann articulated the concept of the body's ability to cure itself in the 19th century. Acupuncturists, Indian shamans, Tibetan monks, charismatics, and even the high priest in the holy Temple of old, were and are still referred to as "healers," but the association obscures the truth and prevents the only valid definition of healing from surfacing. There is only one force of energy that truly heals and that is the Light of the Creator.

All other healing consists of a variety of support mechanisms that permit the unobstructed spiritual Light to perform its duty, which is to search out and destroy harmful foreign bodies and repair, if necessary, the damage inflicted by the darkness of the Opponent. From such minor ailments as back pain, fatigue, and skin rashes to afflictions as serious as cancer, heart disease, and AIDS, the critical factor for a cure is the flow of energy from the spiritual Light.

A sick body is a body with a low-level Light. Illness may result as a direct response to situations of sadness or bereavement in which, as we have seen, the Shechinah abandons the patient, leaving him or her vulnerable to severance from Yesod consciousness. The Shechinah, you will remember, is the metaphysical force that serves as a screen to protect us from the direct power of the Light of the Creator as well as the means by which we make a connection with Yesod consciousness—to vaporize negativity. By connecting with the flow of the spiritual Light, any number of humanity's afflictions can be eliminated. Our immune systems are the key to their eradication and Kabbalistic meditation can make it happen.

We have the ability, in other words, to become our own healers. If we permit it, spiritual Light will flow through us, healing as it moves through our bodies and souls. Yet, at the same time, we labor under the illusion that we may freely interfere with the normal rhythm of bodily functions through negative thought, drug or alcohol abuse, inappropriate medical nostrums, over- or under-eating, or any of the myriad other things we do to the detriment of the heart, liver, kidneys, and other vital organs.

We have essentially two bodies. The first is the illusory physical construct we occupy here in Malchut. The second is a concealed metaphysical body directly connected with the Tree of Life. It serves as an interface between the Tree of Knowledge and the Tree of Life where the only real healing takes place.

Seeing and Believing

Before we examine the actual discipline of Kabbalistic meditation as it pertains to healing, let us first explore a significant self-healing technique that we can incorporate into the process. It is the use of imagery.

The placebo effect is well known in all applications of medicine. To call something a placebo means that its benefits arise from the belief-consciousness of the patient rather than from anything inherent in the medicine itself. The healing that has occurred from placebos proves beyond a doubt that thoughts can trigger the body's own self-healing abilities. Through directed imaging, our beliefs, desires, and resolve to enhance recovery are translated into substantive healing. In short, just as we can deceive ourselves into self-healing because we have been tricked by a placebo, so we can do it deliberately, with an intentional consciousness.

Much research has focused on the connection between mental activity and the physical body, and most of it indicates that the mind actively participates in curing sickness. Kabbalists have always known this. They have engaged in what has popularly come to be called the power of mind over matter, but they take the concept one step further than physical scientists looking into the same phenomenon. The Kabbalist suggests that more than being a mere participant in the metaphysical-quantum scheme, a man or woman, utilizing the power of thought, can determine both physical and metaphysical activity.

To accomplish this, we bring into play the seven Sfirot represented on the Tree of Life schematic (Tikkune Hanefesh-correction of the soul) from Chesed down to Malchut. These energy quanta,

also known as the tetragrammaton, directly affect specific parts
of the body through astral influence.

Tikkune Hanefesh

The top triad in the tree, consisting of Keter, Chochmah, and
Binah, represents the motivating forces that empower and
direct the external senses of sight, sound, smell, and taste. Each
packet governs and influences the two eyes, two ears, two nos-
trils, and the mouth. The Sfirot therefore open the door to
Kabbalistic healing of every part of the body.

To utilize the power of the tetragrammaton, the practitioner simply has to meditate upon the combination of holy names pertinent to the physical area afflicted, then, through kavanah, direct their power to that area. As the most powerful channels of the raw, unshielded power of the Light of the Creator, these names are never to be pronounced, but in healing, they can be meditated upon with complete safety and effectiveness.

The basic idea of using astral forces to influence human life is as old as the human race itself. Ancients recognized the "magic" of light and worshiped the sun, the moon, and other celestial bodies. They understood that astral influences existed, but they could do little to utilize or overcome them. We know now that the effect of light on our minds and bodies is less magical than biological. The healing power of light is a subject of inquiry in clinics and laboratories around the world. Science finally is acknowledging something humans always have instinctively known: light uplifts and energizes; light vaporizes what darkness conceals; light makes us feel good. Science can use light to alter our body clocks, moods, sleep patterns, and possibly even our immune systems. And if light on the physical level can do all that, how much greater are the opportunities when the metaphysical spiritual energy of the Torah is brought to bear?

Before we can heal ourselves, however, we must overcome the obstacles of our own negativity and of grief, sadness, and depression—the foul klippah that covers us and shields us from the all-healing Light of the Creator.

Scientists now are systematically studying bereavement and sadness and their effect on physical health and on the human immune system. They have found that the immune systems of grieving individuals indeed are weakened. But the reason eludes them, as does the mechanism. Most researchers attribute the impact to stress, which is only a label, not an adequate description.

The Zohar attributes the link between grief and the immune system to a disruption of the Yesod consciousness—a disruption stemming from the fact that bereavement and sadness cannot coexist with the Shechinah. And, as discussed earlier, it is the Shechinah that channels spiritual Light to the immune system. The longer the disruption continues, the greater the danger to the immune system because, to function, it requires the sustenance only the Light of the Creator can convey. The immune system is the instrument that marshals a body's defenses against cancer and a host of infectious diseases, but it must be charged with energy to work, and only the Light can do that job. The Opponent, the master of chaos, knows exactly how to keep a gulf of darkness between us and the Light. He does it with stress.

It has long been recognized that stress is a major contributing factor where dis-ease is concerned. Stress paves the way for afflictions ranging from fatal stroke and heart attack to ulcers, which increasingly are reported even in little children. Stress breaks up sleeping patterns, diverts us from positive action, and clouds our lives with anxiety. But, like negative energy, stress, in and of itself, is not "bad."

If a manufacturer rents a loft for an operation, the weight of the machinery that must be installed translates as stress to the floor that must carry it. That stress cannot be eliminated because the machinery is essential. The manager therefore must test the floor to learn what weight it will bear, and if the floor is too weak, it must be reinforced. In the same way, if the "floor" of our lives is too weak to bear the stress of living, then we must reinforce it with the Shechinah.

In order to do that, we must control attitude. Remember, the Shechinah serves as the metaphysical immune system, but it flees from the very sadness and depression that our reaction to stress tends to produce. Therefore, proactively, we must shed the negative mind-set through Kabbalistic meditation techniques covered earlier. The degree of our healing depends entirely upon our ability to restore the inner Light to its fullest revelation, and that can be achieved only by transforming our negative desire to receive for the self alone to a positive attitude of sharing. Only then can we take on any microscopic invaders bent on disrupting the natural balance of our bodies.

The transformation of our inherent desire to receive from one of greed to one of sharing has nothing to do with religion, or even with morality and ethics. It is a matter of supreme self-interest. Any time we behave in a negative fashion, yielding to greed, envy, hatred, and intolerance, we are, in effect, tampering with the natural healing powers within our own bodies. With every negative thought or act, we are putting ourselves at risk. There is only one reason why our society as a whole will become a sharing community and that is because it pays to do so. Religious prohibition of "sin" has very little to do with it. Without the higher consciousness of spiritual Light, we are doomed to walk all our lives on the cyclical treadmill of success-failure, tomorrow-yesterday, health-disease.

We Spoke Too Soon

The complete elimination of all disease is one of the great dreams of humankind, and on the surface our scientific community seems to have made progress toward that goal. The only smallpox bacteria left on Earth now reside in test tubes in four high-security research labs, and devastating plagues of centuries past now are tamed in most of the world by vaccines unimagined at mid-century. We have come so far, so fast, that some medical researchers in the 1980s were predicting that the next couple of decades would constitute little more than a mopping-up operation as we eradicated the few maladies remaining.

In 1990, British fantasy writer Terry Pratchett, in a tale of the *Four Horsemen of the Apocalypse*, changed their names from War, Famine, Pestilence, and Death, to War, Famine, Pollution, and Death on grounds that Pestilence now was passé.

As though infuriated by the snub, Pestilence staged a comeback with a vengeance—and with a horrific new entourage in tow: Ebola, Hantavirus, flesh-eating bacteria, and such bizarre afflictions as Diamond-Blackfan anemia and Labrea black fever. To make matters worse, through overuse of antibiotics, a host of old killers have mutated into new, highly infectious strains immune to penicillin, tetracycline, and vancomycin. They include pneumonia, meningitis, dysentery, food poisoning, tuberculosis, and malaria.

According to the World Health Organization, tuberculosis, once thought nearly extinct, now kills 3 million of the 8.8 million who contract it every year. In 1994, the American Society for Microbiology reported that pneumonia claimed 78,000 victims in the United States, while food poisoning took 9,000 more. Pestilence is back, and it is raging.

We might have known. The notion of a static, healthy human society runs contrary to the development of evolutionary history, which always has been a process of perpetual change. The moment we seem to grasp a solution to one major medical problem, another waits in the wings, ready to make its devastating entrance on the stage of medical history. In an excess of hubris, every generation is sure that it is the one destined to conquer the forces of evil and eradicate all conflict, fight the ultimate "war to end all wars," or win the battle against disease to usher in the age of perpetual health and longevity.

But that goal will remain nothing more than a dream unless we accept the responsibility of achieving our own good health. We must develop a personal determination to participate in the process and do what is required. We can restore ease only though an infusion of spiritual energy, the innate characteristic of which is balance and the perpetual state of which is undisturbed calm. Solutions never will be found by a system that treats surface symptoms; what the Kabbalist strives for is a change in human behavior.

Physician, Heal Thyself

The worst calamities facing humankind are of our own making. Runaway consumption, the degradation of our planet, the poisoning of our oceans, and the fouling of our atmosphere all threaten our crops, our water supply, and consequently, our health. Our recklessness and insensitivity have metastasized to the extent that, from the planet's point of view, we are the main disease in need of elimination.

Because we insist upon treating symptoms and ignoring causes, we have become our own worst enemy, possibly even hastening our own annihilation even as we claim tactical successes on the dis-ease battlefield. The technology that produced advances in production of our food supply included the infusion of antibiotics and hormones now seen as potentially catastrophic. The same technology that has brought about many genuine medical achievements still is unable to control the multiplication of disease strains that have thrown Earth's homeostasis out of balance.

An example of backward thinking in medical science may be found in the Nobel Prize awarded in 1989 to Harold Varmus and J. Michael Bishop of the University of California at San Francisco. The two researchers were honored, and rightly so, for their discovery of cancer-causing oncogenes in humans. Oncogenes are normal genes gone haywire because of mutations or dislocations in the body's DNA. But when Varmus and Bishop set out to correct the situation, their first step was to find where the mistakes in the molecular structure lay. Then, and only then, they said, could science find a means of healing cancer.

Their first question should have been not where the mistakes in DNA lay, but why the mistakes occurred in the first place. One glance at how much is owed to the American medical establishment, which is in the billions and accelerating, should be enough to make one conclude that the problem is not oncogenes running wild. The problem is a medical establishment that is out of control. And, like a metastasizing cancer, the malady is spreading throughout the body politic. Our deficit-ridden system no longer maintains economic stability and balance. Crime and distrust of government are rampant. Our social immune system is as far out of whack as our personal immune systems are. But through the power of Kabbalah, help is at hand. As the next chapter will reveal, it is at our fingertips to regenerate severed limbs and diseased organs, conquer disease, and perhaps even banish death.

CHAPTER 8

BEYOND THE END

In Israel, in order to be a realist, you must believe in miracles.

—David Ben-Gurion, 1886–1973

The Fall of an Illusion

Whether or not you are in Israel, you are about to be asked to believe in miracles. The one we are concerned with was addressed by English poet John Donne more than 300 years ago. Donne wrote:

> *Death be not proud, though some have called thee mighty and dreadful, for thou art not so, For those whom thou think'st thou dost overthrow, Die not, poor death, nor yet canst thou kill me.*

There is no record that Donne, who also observed that "no man is an island," was a Kabbalist, but his views on death and isolation certainly fit with Kabbalistic thinking. In truth, the only people death can "kill" are those who cannot connect with the Tree of Life because they have rejected the Light of the Creator. What seems miraculous to most people is usually quite commonplace in Kabbalah. Let us state it right up front: One who masters Kabbalah need not die, because the spiritual Light is eternal.

The Opponent, ever the trickster, is the one who clothes death in robes of terror, painting a mendacious picture of the skeletal "grim reaper" who carries a scythe the size of a bulldozer blade in his bony hand. The Opponent whispers that death is a dark and inescapable finality—a lonely corridor down which all must walk and none return. As ever, the Opponent is a liar.

Let us take a look at a rather complicated passage from the Zohar dealing with a death that never happened—the death of Jacob, third and greatest of the biblical patriarchs. Because the message of the text is so important, it is repeated here verbatim:

> *Come and see! Jacob is united with the Tree of Life reality, over which death has no dominion, inasmuch as in it, all life is contained. And it provides life to all those who are in perfect union with it. And for this reason, Jacob did not really die. And when he did die, it refers to the metaphor, "and he gathered his legs onto the bed," which means [that] the bed refers to the Tree of Knowledge reality, and when he joined with this reality, he came in contact with the Sitrah Ahrah, the code name for death, and "was gathered unto his people," which means he no longer was in contact with the physical reality.*

It takes a bit of translation, but what it means is simply this: Jacob left the physical environment we call reality only when he chose to do so, and death had nothing to do with it. In fact, the Zohar illustrates a stunning paradox: death exists for the sole purpose of proving that it does not exist. Death negates itself.

Long before his departure from the physicality of Malchut, Jacob had attained the consciousness of the Tree of Life. But because his body remained alive and functional, he was seen here by friends, followers, and members of his extended family. But there is only one exit from the illusory world of Malchut, and that is through the door of the illusion. Therefore, when Jacob decided he no longer desired physical existence, he merely "touched" the Tree of Knowledge—an act implied by the metaphor of gathering his legs onto the bed—in order to stop the heartbeat of the body he no longer cared to inhabit. At that moment, those gathered at his bedside saw what seemed to be a living body becoming a corpse, which they no doubt buried with great weeping and lamentation.

The scene, clearly viewed by Jacob from his unaltered position in the Tree of Life reality, must have seemed bizarre, no more than people wailing over a tattered old coat that had been thrown out to make room in the wardrobe for a new one.

To those left behind, in the Tree of Knowledge reality, Jacob "vanished" into the grave. To Jacob, in the Tree of Life reality, it was those left behind who ultimately vanished. Death, a revelation showing us that there is no death, thus becomes the greatest illusion of all. Death is not a skeleton wrapped in a shroud; death is a door through which we pass into the realm of truth. Unfortunately, convinced that death is real, most of us go right on "touching the bed" in a desperate, if misguided, effort to go on "living." As a result, nonexistent death is the only thing that interests us, and our lives are blighted as a result.

When one achieves communion with the energy of the Tree of Life reality, chaos no longer remains a part of the human landscape. When thus connected, we are allowed to reject death. This viewpoint will require a complete overhaul of the average person's perspective concerning chaos and death, but all we need to eliminate chaos from our lives is a change in consciousness. Chaos, ill health, financial failure, and all the rest of the Opponent's dismal litany will be seen for what they are—illusory manifestations of mind and consciousness. In short, when that is realized on a broad scale, the Opponent finally will be conquered. If we achieve this change of consciousness, we will be prepared for the Light of the Creator and its ability to enlighten us and illuminate the dark corridors of our lives.

The Recurring Miracle

In modern hospitals, it does happen that patients declared clinically dead actually return to life. But the Kabbalist goes a step further. If life can be restored to the dead, why not apply the same metaphysical miracle to restoration of a severed limb or failing organ? If a lizard can lose its tail and grow another one, what is to keep a human, who is a quantum leap up on the evolutionary scale, from accomplishing the same kind of feat? The DNA that formed the limb in the first place is still there; why can the human brain not command it to repeat the process? The answer is that the brain can do just that, but we have been conditioned to doubt it, and doubt poisons all endeavors. But before we consider the phenomenon of regeneration further, let us first address the question of immortality.

Biblical reports of immortality go well beyond the story of Jacob. No one can find the grave of Moses in Sinai. Enoch and Elijah are said to have been transported directly to heaven, and the prophet Ezekiel raised a whole valley full of "dry bones," fleshing them out into vital human beings again. Even Rabbi Shimon bar Yohai is said to have brought two sages, named R. Yosi of Pe'quin and R. Isaac, back from the dead.

The cynic will sneer that such reports and beliefs are mythological folk tales inspired by little more than wishful thinking, but in metaphysical terms, that is far too simplistic.

Physical immortality exists now, just as it has from the beginning. We do not see it because we have given the mundane dominion over our understanding, and so the Tree of Life is concealed. Conscious awareness that the Tree of Life really does exist for us is the prerequisite for understanding how immortality can be attained. The next step is meditation upon the necessary combinations of Hebrew letters, and most particularly upon the 72 Names of God.

To know what we are up against, let us consider death from a physical, rather than strictly from a metaphysical, standpoint. Death is the offspring of two soul-mated forces, gravity and entropy, and the Kabbalist knows that the genesis of each is nothing more than the desire to receive for the self alone. If that desire universally could be neutralized through conversion to a desire to receive for the sake of sharing, then both gravity and entropy would cease to exist. And so would the limitations of time, space, and motion. Such material constructs as tables, clothing, bridges, roads, and skyscrapers no longer would be vulnerable to the second law of thermodynamics, which states that all physical matter ultimately must wind down, decay, and come to an end. Imagine an interstate highway system immune to potholes or a building with no requirement for maintenance! And that is not all a world devoid of entropy will bring.

The only reason for the physical body to undergo pain, suffering, degeneration, aging, and death is the Opponent's control over the material universe. In fact, his consciousness, which is desire to receive for the self alone, can be made manifest only when material is involved. Eliminate the Opponent and we eliminate all those debilitating conditions. Imagine a body that never ages, never grows fat, never suffers pain, and never dies!

Rabbi Shimon wrote some 2,000 years ago that the world would slumber in ignorance and darkness for two millennia before it was possible to raise human consciousness to a level of universal awareness. That period finally has arrived and when a majority of the world's inhabitants have raised their consciousness to one of sharing, both immortality and the regeneration of severed limbs and failing organs will be obtained on a wide scale. And because the reversal from greed to sharing is proceeding as never before, that will happen in just a few more years.

That Old Demon Doubt

You may well ask, if these marvels are available, and if increasing numbers of men and women all over the world are raising their consciousnesses toward the Tree of Life reality and removing Bread of Shame from their lives, why are undertakers, transplant surgeons, and the makers of prosthetic limbs still in business?

They are in business simply because even the most enlightened among us believe they have to be. Rabbi Isaac Luria, the Lion of Safed, or the Ari, as he is known, revealed one of Kabbalah's most important doctrines when he stated that negative thoughts ultimately create all of the chaos in our lives. And of all the negative thoughts possible, doubt may be the deadliest.

The reason amputated limbs do not routinely grow back, the reason a cancerous liver or a failing heart do not heal themselves, the reason we all die, is doubt. The same doubt that kept Einstein from walking through his locked door even though he accepted the proposition in theory, is what keeps most of us declaring the return of a severed limb nothing short of a miracle. The fault lies in our consciousness. We do not fundamentally believe such things are possible, and in this illusion-haunted realm of the drawn Light, where chaos is so firmly entrenched in our minds, doubt simply turns out the Light. Our minds have been programmed to reject a cancer cure, a resurrection, or the possibility that a lost arm or leg might regrow itself, even though, in the latter case, it never truly disappeared in the first place.

That statement is not as outrageous as it might seem at first glance. We are conditioned to believe that what we cannot see, cannot possibly be there. But in the Tree of Life, which is as much a glyph of the human body as of the universe, there is no lack. As a result, a limb severed in the physical universe of the Tree of Knowledge remains intact and functional in the second body, which dwells within the concealed Light of the Tree of Life. This is the metaphysical phenomenon that gives rise to the phantom limb syndrome, in which amputees actually feel an itch that they cannot scratch or a pain they cannot soothe in the lost limb.

Why Just a "Phantom?"

Logically, why should a severed limb not regenerate itself? The DNA—the genetic blueprint that put the arm or the leg there in the first place—has not changed. The physical capability remains. Hair and fingernails grow when cut; why not arms and legs?

The only difference between the healing of a broken limb and the regeneration of a severed one is consciousness. Our eyes can observe the knitting of a broken bone; therefore, we have entered into a consciousness that admits the bone can be healed. This, in fact, may be the very reason why it is healed. Try giving up on it, saying it is "too far gone," and the chances of its mending will be greatly diminished.

Most people still believe that what we cannot see, hear, feel, smell, or taste simply does not exist, but this concept is an out-dated legacy from Newton and the physical science of his day. Finally the scientists are beginning to march to the Kabbalistic drumbeat. The classical physics question asks, "If a tree falls in the forest and no one is there to hear it, does it make a sound?" The answer is, "Of course it does; by creating pressure waves in the air, it makes a sound whether anyone is there to hear it or not." Quantum mechanics disagrees.

In the view of the quantum physicist, the tree is a construct of consciousness and therefore it exists only when we perceive it. If matter does not become material until the observer observes it, we should be able simply to refuse to look at a cancerous tumor, thus causing it to fade out of existence. But this is where the Kabbalist and the physicist part company. The Zohar has established dual levels of reality. They are the concealed Light, reserved for those who have removed Bread of Shame and entered into the Tree of Life, and the drawn Light, which governs our rational consciousness in this material world. The physicist claims no ability to alter the physicality of the drawn

Light reality, but the Kabbalist can and will remove a cancerous tumor, since the tumor belongs to the chaotic reality of the drawn Light. Like its equivalent, the seemingly missing limb, the tumor belongs to the reality of the Tree of Knowledge.

As the new millennium begins, those of us who strive to alter our states of consciousness actually will begin to experience the so-called miracles discussed here. As each person becomes aware of his or her ability to change not only personal destiny, but that of the world, then a collective consciousness will emerge in support of a healthy society. This society, in turn, will strongly assist the rapid improvement of personal health, finances, and relationships for the entire community. Spiritual Light is a constant companion within the biological framework of humankind. When we permit it to infuse our corporeal bodies with the life-giving force of energy, we all will begin to enjoy the benefits of the Creator's original intent toward His Creation, which is to share His eternal beneficence and life.

With that established, we now must look into the role both consciousness and knowledge will play in the new world now dawning.

CHAPTER 9

CONSCIOUSNESS AND CREATION

The universe begins to look more like a great thought than like a great machine.

– *British scientist Sir James Jeans, 1877–1946.*

All and Everything

Consciousness, the essential stuff of all material existence, is all the reality that ever was or ever will be. Positive consciousness is the Light of the Creator, with all the beneficence He offers his Creation. Negative consciousness, on the other hand, is responsible for all the pain and suffering endured by the human race. Any time any one of us is guilty of negative activity, that person invites the Opponent to come calling. It doesn't take much of an effort to let him in. The Opponent lives in the narrowest cracks of darkness and he can invade our lives through the tiniest of openings. Unfortunately, we usually give him one the size of a barn door.

One of the Opponent's best stratagems is to lull us into a failure to recognize the power of human consciousness. We have been led to believe—especially by the scientific establishment— that our consciousness is separated from the physical world and thus has no direct bearing on what we perceive as reality. But that is just another of the Opponent's lies. Everything in the physical domain, terrestrial and celestial, is merely an interference pattern, described by Sir James Jeans in *Mysterious Universe*, as little more than "an impertinent blip in the world of thought." Under the nearly metaphysical prodding of quantum mechanics, the scientist finally is beginning to recognize that there is more knowledge and consciousness in the construction of the universe than ever was dreamed of in classical physics.

Take the familiar optical illusion of the drawing of two human profiles, facing each other.

When seen in one way, the space between the profiles appears to be a goblet; looked at another way, the goblet becomes two profiles again. Mentally, we easily can grasp the fact that both views exist at once, but we are incapable of encompassing both realities at the same time. This simple example should convince us that physical reality really is just an illusion, depending completely upon the state of our consciousness at any given time.

Every particle in our universe represents a unique energy intelligence, and the number of such particles runs to infinity. A computer capable of processing 50 billion units of information per second could not begin to complete the inventory. There are just too many of them for science to corral into equations that might permit the prediction of future cosmic events.

The human brain is equally staggering. It houses hundreds of billions of energy intelligences, their multiple interconnections equally defiant of quantification. Therefore, it is impossible for scientists to use them to predict human behavior.

Kabbalah, alone, has the means of doing so, both on a personal and on a cosmic level, but until the emergence of quantum mechanics and the parallels it presents in the physical universe, there was no way to teach the metaphysical principles of Kabbalah to humankind at large. They were just too abstruse to be grasped by any save a Talmudic scholar with years of study. But the time for Kabbalistic ideas for the general community has arrived.

I See, Therefore It Is

A Kabbalist couple wanted to build an extra room onto their house to accommodate their growing family, but the money for such construction simply wasn't there. Another couple might have sighed, reflected upon how unfair life can be, and given up, but not our Kabbalists. They knew the addition already existed because of their desire, and that all they had to do was make it manifest. Therefore, they started including the project in their daily meditation—not as any formal kind of prayer, but as reflection upon a deed already done. They then carried the theme into the mundane affairs of their life by "seeing" the room every time they walked out the door against which it would be built. In their mind's eye, they made it complete, right down to the carpeting on the floor, the paper on the walls, and every detail of furniture that it would contain. So intense was this visualization that the room became, for them, an integral part of the house. And then, it happened. In rapid order, they received a small inheritance, an income tax return, and an unexpected bonus in connection with their work. With no effort beyond that exercised by their minds, they had the money, and the long-dreamed-of room soon became a reality.

So, one might ask, if it is that easy, why isn't everyone doing it? The answer is that our minds, for the most part, are not connected. Society, which is controlled by the Opponent, has seen to that. Thanks to a lifetime of conditioning that makes us live the same day over and over again for 70 years and prods us into a pattern of repetitive thinking, we don't even try.

In order to construct the metaphysical fences that shut us in, the Opponent uses fragmentation—a force that keeps us from achieving the quantum ability to see things from the perspective of the true reality. Tomorrow is separated from yesterday by the present. How can any of our best-laid plans succeed when we are cut off from tomorrow? How can we prepare for any future undertaking when time and space dominate our existence and prevent us from being in two places at the same time?

The process of fragmentation also extends to our understanding of the five senses. We accept as fact the proposition that our eyes cannot hear or our ears see, but, in a dim reflection of true reality, we constantly strive for some measure of unity. How often do we hear or say, "Look at me when I talk to you," or "Do you read me?" or, "I see what you mean." We fail to remember that thought always precedes the physical; no physical manifestation ever comes about without prior thought consciousness.

Desire Dictates the Deed

The difficulty lies in our stubborn attachment to a reactive state of mind, constantly dominated by our desire to receive for the self alone. We have, for the most part, abandoned our innate ability to share. This surrender has blocked development of a proactive mind and kept us from maintaining the causative state of mind that literally can do anything. Only the proactive can exercise the old Latin motto, *carpe diem*, which means "seize the day."

Take for example a businessman who, due to stock fluctuations and unexpected setbacks in the marketplace, is unpleasantly surprised by a call from his banker.

"You have just written a five-figure check, and there are insufficient funds in your account to cover it," the banker tells him. "What are you going to do about this?"

If the man is reactive, he answers in panic, fielding the ball and fumbling it in his own court. "Oh no!" he gasps. "I'm so sorry. There must be some mistake. Please don't make this public. My future depends on that check; please, please honor it. I'll get the money, I promise you."

But if the man is proactive, he puts the ball firmly back in the banker's court. "I have more than enough funds to cover that check," he tells the banker. "You had better assemble your staff and find out who has made this mistake and if you don't clear this check immediately, you're the one who will be in trouble. When the check clears, then I'll decide if I want to continue doing business with you."

Note that in neither case has the man in question stopped to check his books or call his accountant to learn if, in fact, his bank balance is sufficient to cover the check. But in the first instance, the businessman is in trouble, while in the second instance, the banker is in trouble. The only difference between the two is mind over matter. The proactive man has changed the situation with nothing more than his will.

There is no great mystery here. Intuitively, we know how it works. Consider the bowler who sends the ball sailing down the alley toward the pins, then spends the next few seconds twisting her body into the contortions of "body English" as she guides the ball by sheer dint of will into the one-two pocket that will produce a strike. That is how deeply ingrained the concept of mind over matter is in all of us. And what the bowler, herself, generally dares not really believe is this: mind over matter works.

Proactively, there is no sequence of events in the bowler's actions. The pins, the ball, and the one throwing it all are inextricably interlinked in a single unit of creative consciousness, and since the bowler is in no way truly separated from the ball, she can indeed control its trajectory right up until the moment of impact.

This assertion is no breakthrough; the Zohar revealed it 2,000 years ago when Rabbi Shimon bar Yohai wrote that physical entities and the outcome of events actually are created by desire and thought in a process drawn from the Tree of Life. "In prayers (or meditation), it is necessary to have the desire and the thought to direct consciousness to its ultimate destination," he wrote. He asserted that desire and thought together, controlled by kavanah, can materialize anything. The universe lies at your fingertips. All you have to do is reach out and take it. You are not helpless.

To illustrate the full meaning of the Zohar, let us assume for a moment that, for reasons that are immaterial here, a person decides to break a window. Reactively, the act would seem to be one of utter simplicity: the person simply picks up a stone, takes aim, and lets fly. Classical physics and common sense would say the stone, once picked up and thrown, proceeds along a ballistic curve affected by gravity and atmospheric friction to strike and shatter the frangible glass, leaving nothing more to discuss than a probable summoning of police or, depending on the level of consciousness of the window's owner, a fistfight.

But that is not how a Kabbalist would describe the action. The Kabbalist knows that the stone did not break the window—consciousness did. In fact, the glass shattered before the stone even touched it. A Kabbalistic interpretation would say that when the individual decides to break the window, this thought energy immediately is materialized by consciousness into the energy of the arm, which, in turn, materializes the stone. But it is the original consciousness that breaks the windowpane, not the stone, because material is illusory. This is what The Ari, Rabbi Isaac Luria, meant when he wrote some 400 years ago that consciousness is, in itself, the only reality.

Science Plays Catch-Up

The Ari taught that consciousness is materialized whenever a person wishes to express it. The assertion thus presaged 20th century scientific experiments proving that a windowpane targeted for breaking actually begins to shatter before the stone strikes it, even without the intervention of the arm or the stone, both of which are only the physical manifestations of an already existing reality.

The Ari further states that consciousness, unlike material, never undergoes entropy. As a result, if, in the example of breaking the window, a bird suddenly flies into the path of the stone, diverting it from its target, the thought consciousness to break the pane remains forever unless the individual actively withdraws it. In short, sooner or later, that window is going to be broken because the thought consciousness to break it will remain a real and definitive force. This proposition raises another of the fascinating paradoxes Kabbalah loves to address. Because the thought of the whole, undamaged window is eternal, since the physical windowpane constitutes only an illusory one percent of its existence while the remaining 99 percent is consciousness, it cannot be destroyed because consciousness is immortal.

While the metaphor of stone and windowpane are illustrative of the power of mind over matter, to a Kabbalist the distinction is academic. No Kabbalist would expend energy for so useless a reason. If the motive for breaking a window in the first place is anger at the window's owner, perhaps for an injury real or perceived, the Kabbalist would not react with violence. Being proactive, he or she would approach the offender, seek redress, and settle the matter mentally. To attack the window would be an abuse of energy, and wherever there is an abuse of energy it is in a reactive state under which only the Opponent profits. If all of humankind were proactive, there never would be an abuse of energy and the Opponent, with his chaos, would cease to exist.

For four centuries, The Ari's outlandish notion that a proactive consciousness can create and control was dismissed by scientist and layperson alike as akin to the ancient hairsplitting argument about how many angels could dance on the head of a pin. Then, in the 1980s, two physicists in Switzerland went to work on an obscure study done some 30 years earlier in Esaki, Japan. Experiments there had indicated that a pane of glass targeted by a flying stone really will break before the stone touches it because of a tunnel effect. The Esaki theory held that when two bodies come near each other, charges—mostly electrons—flow from the surface of one to the other before they actually make contact. Thought, of course, is also essentially a flow of electrons along neurons of the brain, directed by the intent of the thinker. The Esaki study suggests that, indeed, it is thought consciousness that breaks the windowpane.

The Esaki study generally was ignored because, according to the laws of classical physics, such a transfer of charges should be impossible. But physicists Heinrich Rohrer and Gerd Binnig, working at IBM in Rueschlikon, Switzerland, some four decades later, finally proved the point by inventing a scanning tunneling microscope that allowed them actually to observe the flow of electric charges. The device proved that as one surface approaches the other, atoms in these surfaces are actually moved about, and the surfaces restructured (i.e., shattered, in the case of the glass), as a result of the energy exchange.

That we radiate energy no longer is in question. The Talmud revealed the fact 2,000 years ago, and now the discovery by the Swiss scientists working on the tunnel effect has established that every human body generates a personal electromagnetic field about 88 inches in diameter. Not only can it affect radio reception, but it also may explain why, when another person violates our "space," he or she either attracts or repels us. A positive, upbeat person can energize us simply by being in the same room, while a negative, hostile soul drains our energy and leaves us in despair. Young people, who re-create language as they go, came up with an unscientific, but thoroughly proper, term for the phenomenon: "vibes."

The breakthrough on the tunnel effect and its resulting understanding of electronic forces as they operate between bodies in proximity won a Nobel Prize for Rohrer and Binnig in 1986. It also provided a metaphysical chance for the spirit of the Ari to smile across the ages and say, "I told you so."

As the Parent Thinks, So Grows the Child

The Ari drew his conclusions about the reality of consciousness from a Zohar commentary on the biblical story of Cain and Abel, which, as a metaphor, is equally appropriate today. When Adam, at the instigation of the serpent through Eve, ate of the forbidden fruit from the Tree of Knowledge, he became attached to the flawed spirit symbolized by the serpent. As a result, upon expulsion from Eden, Eve gave birth to Cain, who, coming from this flawed DNA sequence, was intrinsically evil. Only after Adam repented his original sin was Abel born, from a purified DNA sequence.

What emerges from the Zohar is the role consciousness plays in the creation and development of humankind. In this light, the Kabbalist's understanding that the thinking process converts knowledge to energy should come as no surprise. We already have understood that the structure of matter is not independent of consciousness. Nor is the acquisition of knowledge merely a transfer of information from one source to another. The roots of knowledge run far deeper than the intercourse between teacher and student. Knowledge is more than just a convenient method of achieving a union between human intellects at the highest levels. Knowledge is the origin of all consciousness, and the conscious mind becomes activated through the accumulation of knowledge.

The Zohar expresses this very profound phenomenon by explicating the verse in Genesis that says, "And Adam knew Eve and she gave birth to Cain." People have interpreted this to be a kind of polite evasion—as if the Torah was afraid to speak about sex directly. But the Zohar interprets the verse as a revelation that knowledge—or knowing—indeed is the connection. Knowing is exactly the consciousness that materializes the sperm and egg in creation of another individual, and that happens today every time a baby is conceived.

This is why the thoughts and the mental attitude of the parents at the moment of conception generally determines what sort of individual will be formed of their union. If their thoughts and feelings during intercourse are charged with love and kindness, those attributes will be carried over to the child. But if their union is one of anger, brutality, and lust, the child formed of that union most likely will inherit those negative characteristics. That is why two seemingly wonderful parents sometimes produce a child that is the epitome of evil. That is why Cain, whose conception was tainted by the serpent of the Tree of Knowledge, murdered his brother, Abel.

Human DNA is not, after all, the origin of a human being. It is only part of a process begun in the consciousness of the father and mother—a consciousness that alone has the power to materialize the physical DNA. Only when two parents share love and admiration for each other can that DNA emerge free of the corruption of the Tree of Knowledge. Only then can the perfect structure of Tree of Life DNA sequences emerge.

There are infinite combinations of DNA in the Tree of Life, and whatever attributes ultimately become manifest in the child will resemble parents and grandparents only to the extent that negative thoughts and feelings are avoided in the course of that child's conception. If would-be parents only knew this, it would serve to put romance back in marriage and result in far less metaphysical damage to offspring. Consciousness is all the reality that ever was or ever will be. It is what produces and becomes the essential stuff of all material existence.

The Poison of Doubt

Anyone who ever saw the Cecil B. DeMille movie epic, The Ten Commandments, knows what a trial the job of leading the Israelites out of Egypt was for Moses. In fact, he didn't lead them at all—he dragged them, kicking, screaming, whining, and complaining all the way. Every time the going got tough, which was most of the time, they wailed in self-pity and nagged Moses to take them back to slavery in Egypt, where they at least had three square meals a day and a roof over their heads at night.

It is no wonder, then, that Moses lost his temper over the matter of drawing water from the stone. It was a particularly hot, dry day; and there was no water for the congregation; and they assembled against Moses and Aaron, and the people fought with Moses and said, "Better would it have been that we perished together with our fellow Jews before the Lord. Why have you brought the assembly of the Lord into this desert so that we and our cattle will die here? Why did you take us out of Egypt, to bring us to this evil place?"

This was a crowd that had witnessed one miracle after another, from the parting of the Red Sea with the rod Moses carried to the fall of manna when they were starving, and still they could say only, "Well, sure, but what have you done for me lately?"

Miracles alone are not enough to raise consciousness. The Israelites were not convinced that they could master the power of nature and they obviously were in the mood for a lynching on that hot, dry, waterless day. Thoroughly vexed, and more than a little afraid, Moses took the matter to the Lord:

And the Lord said unto Moses, "Take the rod and assemble the congregation, you and Aaron, your brother, and you should speak to the rock before their eyes and it will give forth its water, and you shall bring forth to them water out of the rock". . . And Moses and Aaron assembled the congregation before the rock and he said unto them: "Hear now you rebels; are we to bring forth water out of this rock?" And Moses lifted up his hand and smote the rock with his rod twice; and water came forth abundantly and the congregation drank and also their cattle.

And with that action, Moses lost his ticket to the Promised Land. Once before, he had been told to strike a rock and bring forth water, but this time he had been instructed to "speak" to it, not hit it with his staff, and the Creator took it personally. "Because you did not believe in Me, to sanctify Me (make me whole) in the eyes of the children of Israel," the Lord told him, "therefore you shall not bring this assembly into the land which I have given to them." And, the Lord added, "Aaron would not be allowed to make the trip, either."

It was a harsh punishment and a story that, taken at face value, would seem to cast the Almighty less as Creator of the universe than as a peevish parent grounding His offspring forever over a relatively minor infraction. But, never forget, the Bible has many layers. It is more than just a series of stories; it is the code of the universe and Kabbalah is its deciphering instrument. Beneath the narrative of Moses and the stone lie codes of knowledge that tell a far more important story.

Sages and scholars have debated the meaning of those codes for centuries and we will go into a few of their interpretations here where they involve the question of mind over matter, but one simple truth must be stated from the beginning. Moses did what he did because of doubt—that of the negative multitude that surrounded him, and his own. He knew he was supposed to draw water from the rock simply by speaking combinations of the 72 Names of God, thus illustrating to his recalcitrant followers the power of thought consciousness and of energy. But he was drowning in a sea of hostility and doubt.

Having seen firsthand what Moses could do with the rod, the Israelites were prepared to believe in its power, but they balked at the thought that merely speaking the Names of God could produce such a miracle. They simply could not come to grips with the concept of mind over matter. Moses "smote" the rock because he feared if he did otherwise their doubt would overwhelm him and the miracle would be stopped in its tracks.

But, in using the rod as a guarantee that doubt on the part of the congregation would not cancel the miracle and prevent the flow of water, Moses blew a fuse in the circuitry of the Tree of Life, and that is what barred him from ever seeing the Promised Land. He hoped the gap of doubt would be bridged by the rod, but doubt can only be bridged by consciousness. By attempting to gull his followers into belief, Moses lost the opportunity to raise the consciousness of the Israelites to an understanding of the true nature and power of that proactive consciousness.

Now You See It, Now You Don't

Like the Israelites of the Exodus, we find great difficulty in believing or accepting the principle that there is nothing to reality apart from consciousness. Physical, material reality is nothing but the vehicle by which consciousness is expressed. This has been the nature of our universe ever since Adam opted for the Tree of Knowledge and its universal illusory reality.

The vast majority of us live our daily lives in a reactive state of mind. There are very few individuals who can be considered proactive, which is to say, not affected by outside influences or the environment. An employee's actions are subject to the demands of the employer. We dress in clothes dictated by designers and manufacturers; we live in ways that society directs. Advertising formulates our tastes and desires. For the most part, our lives are governed by outside influences. Even the ideas of rebellious individuals can usually be traced to problems with ego and do not necessarily reflect independence or individualism. In most cases, rebellion is just another form of reaction to authority, a desire to express individuality that is not at all synonymous with being proactive. Real proactivism is not responsive to such outside influences as authority, advertising, or societal propaganda.

Humankind alone has been given the ability—it might even be said, the burden—to reveal the Light of the Creator. The illusion of darkness, pain, and suffering comprises only a tiny fraction of the cosmic picture. But the vast majority of people live in and experience only the illusion. Where there is Light, they see and feel darkness; where there is good, they see evil; where there is truth, they see only fiction. The Opponent, the master of illusion, sees to that.

He was there in the desert with Moses, whispering to the Israelites, "It can't be done; it's all a lie; don't let him make fools of you," and by so doing, he drove them to overwhelm even Moses with their negativity. Today, the Opponent has programmed the collective mind of humankind with the idea that only the physical, material reality represents the universe as we observe it. In our world, consciousness has been relegated to the backseat and physical reality has become the driver. Our culture celebrates the athletes, movie stars, and moguls who have mastered the art of financial accumulation, not those for whom bringing knowledge and light to the world is of the utmost importance.

The Golden Calf

Deification of an idol is nothing new. It happened on a grand and arcane scale some 3,000 years ago while Moses was atop Mount Sinai receiving the Ten Commandments. Moses' problems with his fretful Israelite charges stemmed from the fact that their consciousness, locked into slavery through generations, was incapable of handling freedom or freedom's price, which is responsibility. Moses' mission was to raise their collective consciousness, lead them to the Light of the Creator, and craft a nation from their ranks.

To accomplish this, he was drawn to Mount Sinai where, in history's first summit conference, he received from the Lord, firsthand, the revelation of the Decalogue and a compendium of other lifestyle instructions that persist to this day. In the course of these events, the formal religion of Judaism was born, but it did not happen overnight.

Since Moses, alone, could face the raw, surging, energy of the Almighty without being consumed by it, he was forced to approach the power center alone, leaving the Israelites to their own devices. Given the level of their emotional maturity, that was the equivalent of leaving 600,000 five-year-olds unattended in a Toys"R"Us warehouse. Mischief was bound to happen, and it did.

Having decided, after 40 days of grumbling and self-pity, that their leader and the Lord alike had abandoned them in the desert, the Israelites strong-armed Aaron, high priest and Moses' brother, into manufacturing a new "God" to lead them out of the desert. We are told in Exodus that Aaron—always a bit of a weathercock in the willpower department—caved in to the idolatrous demand and confiscated all the gold earrings the Israelites had brought with them out of Egypt. These were melted down into a molten mass from which a golden calf was formed. The people quickly deified the idol, proclaiming it a "God" that had brought them out of Egypt, and celebrated the occasion with an early version of sex, drugs, and rock and roll. The party ended abruptly when Moses unexpectedly returned. With the stone tablets he had gotten from the Lord, he smashed the idol and executed the perpetrators. Called on the carpet by Moses, Aaron could only mumble that, forced by the people, he took some gold, threw it into the fire, "and this calf came out." In short: "It's not my fault; I couldn't help it; I don't know how it happened, the Devil made me do it." Some things never change.

The Real Story

That is the narrative version of the story, but the underlying truth, revealed in the Zohar, is much deeper and more complex. The biblical account doesn't mention them specifically, but some pretty sinister characters, versed in some pretty sinister practices, came out of Egypt with the children of Israel. They are what is known in the Zohar as the Erev Rav—Jews trained in the practice of Egyptian sorcery and consumed with the desire to receive for the self alone. Because they were steeped in a corrupted version of the Tree of Life, their metaphysical powers almost equaled those that Moses had learned to wield.

The Egyptians practiced a very real magic. It was not the sort displayed by the stage illusionist who, by sleight of hand, appears to pull a rabbit out of a hat or saw a beautiful lady in two, yet leave her in one piece. They derived their power through domination only of the negative, left-hand column of the Tree of Knowledge. Then, by intensifying their desire to receive to the level of rapacity, they went beyond what the Zohar calls the 49th gate of uncleanness. Details of that corrupted system cannot be dealt with here in full; suffice to say that the 49th gate represents a total sellout to the Opponent—in short, a soul so consumed by desire to receive for the self alone that it is beyond all hope of redemption.

The Erev Rav were a distillate of corruption, but their skills could not be denied. They had, among other things, perfected the art of embalming to a level still admired today by those who study their culture. They were, in short, masters of death and, as Moses quickly discovered, they could match him miracle for miracle by concentrating the negativity of the left-hand column into pure, palpable evil.

Yunus and Yumbrus were two of the darkest of these magicians. Though trained by Egyptian priests, they were Jews and, as such, presumably had been forced to accompany the Israelite horde out of Egypt. In all probability, they were not happy about that, and it may be guessed that they had waited a long time for Moses to turn his back on them so that they could seize his power. With Moses gone, they were the ones who whipped up the disaffected among the Israelites to clamor for a "new God." And, with Yunus and Yumbrus at the helm, the Israelites were given a nightmare of a "God." More than just a golden idol, like some eerie creation from the hand of a prototypical Frankenstein, the golden calf could breathe, move, and speak. Offered this mechanistic marvel, the Israelites found it easy to forget the true miracles they had seen—especially since Yunus and Yumbrus threw in an orgy as a bonus.

Don't Try This at Home

Despite the surface meaning of the biblical narrative, Yunus and Yumbrus needed no golden earrings from the rank and file of Moses' followers to make their miracle. Because gold, by its very nature, is an element of the left column, the two Erev Rav were able to draw it down, effectively creating gold out of nothing. But, since they had no computer-generated graphics or animatronic technology with which to imbue the metal with life, they needed more. That is where Aaron came into the picture.

As high priest of the Israelites, Aaron was a direct representative of the Sfira of Chesed, the expansive energy packet of mercy on the right column of the Tree of Life. Chesed, on the positive pole of Tree of Life circuitry, imparts total desire to receive for the sake of sharing, while its negative counterpart, Gvurah, on the left column, represents restriction, and consequently, a desire to receive that, without balance, easily is converted to desire to receive for the self alone. Furthermore, Chesed contains only the essence of things and events that take their first step toward corporeality in Gvurah.

Yunus and Yumbrus, using the Tree of Knowledge, which is a corrupted mirror image of the Tree of Life, had access to Gvurah, but without Aaron's input, they could not touch Chesed. Without Chesed, where the potentiality of life resides, their idol could not live.

The Zohar tells us Yunus and Yumbrus "handed" the gold to Aaron who, instead of working it with a chisel as the narrative account says, actually put it "in a sack" where none of the multitude could see what was about to happen to it. Remember the power of the poison of doubt. The Israelites wallowed in it, and the two wily magicians knew that its collective force could short-circuit what they were about to do. Therefore, even as stage magicians today divert their audience's eyes from their hands as they prepare to pull a rabbit out of a hat, they make sure that what is about to happen will happen in darkness. One cannot doubt what one cannot perceive.

Yunus and Yumbrus needed Aaron and his right column connection, because, as explained earlier, everything in the universe emerges from Chesed to become manifest in Gvurah. In the case of the golden calf, the gold emerged from the left column as a differentiated substance, which the magicians then gave to Aaron, who "embraced" it, unwittingly imbuing it with the internal energy of Chesed.

As previously stated, gold is a left-column element, with negative energy. By removing its physically manifested sequence to the pure energy intelligence of the left column, the magicians wound up with an entity of raw, naked, left-column energy to which they could attach another metaphysical DNA sequence. This new sequence produced a new physical manifestation—a golden calf in the form of "a living God."

Even in Moses' day, though it would not be discovered for 3,000 years, the double helix of DNA existed, directing the formulation of every living thing from algae to humankind. DNA was, and is, represented by Chesed, the Sfira of undifferentiated potential. In such latter-day animated mechanical wonders as robots and computers, DNA can be thought of as a series of silicon chips. And, like the evolution of fetus to baby or software program to usable computer function, the proper circuitry must be in place to animate it.

Kabbalistically, that circuitry involves the internal, left-column energy, which is where the expression of the Light takes place. Within a state of right-column energy or consciousness, the Light is in a potential, motionless state, transcending the limits of time, space, or motion. But if the Light becomes enveloped by a left-column energy force, it responds to the desire of the vessel and moves from the potential state of Chesed to the actual state of Gvurah. That is how the golden calf came into existence, and had the process been reversed, rolling the object back from manifestation to potential, it would have been unmade as swiftly as it was created.

These concepts are not easy, but they cannot be written off as a matter of myth. Use of spiritual Light in this fashion constitutes a prime example of mind over matter and, with the dawning of the 21st century, we will see more and more examples of it. As the collective consciousness of the human race further is raised, science will come to realize that it is possible to eliminate a physical entity or material expression, such as a cancerous tumor, by rolling it back to its original positive or right-column state of potentiality. Even now, science is on the cusp of learning that other sequences can be cloned, and these clones will achieve the raw, naked energy necessary to accomplish things hitherto only dreamed of. Indeed, in our time, ordinary people will walk in Eden's garden, achieve flawless health, and fly to the stars, all with nothing more than the whisper of a thought.

CHAPTER 10

DANGEROUS INTENTIONS

From ghoulies and ghosties and long-leggety beasties and things that go bump in the night, Good Lord, deliver us!

—*Cornish prayer*

A Solar System NASA Never Sees

The furthest extension of the idea that all is consciousness and consciousness is all is expressed in Kabbalistic astrology. Entire volumes have been written on this subject. Its full scope is far beyond the purview of this book, but because the astrological aspect plays such an important role and because Kabbalistic astrology is so much different than the commonly known variety, it must at least be introduced here.

Unlike their counterparts in conventional astrology, the planets and signs of the Kabbalistic zodiac are living, conscious intelligences. While they compel us to do absolutely nothing, they definitely impel us in almost everything, and by so doing, provide us with energies specific to our need of removing chaos from our lives. The task of the Kabbalist is to understand the forces of the zodiac and use them to gain a thorough knowledge of and connection with nature, with the universe, and with each person's place in it. "As above, so below," says the Zohar, and with the help of the Aleph Bet, Kabbalistic astrologers have seen the intimate connection between the life of humans and the life of the universe as a whole. This is the true significance of the words in Genesis, "And the Lord created man in His own image; in the image of the Lord created He him."

Kabbalistic astrology is a far cry from the over-generalized drivel in the daily newspaper or the cliche, "What's your sign?" To date, for all our technological advances, the only place beyond Mother Earth where humans actually have walked is the moon. We have sent robotic probes to Venus, Mars, and the gas giants of the outer solar system, but Kabbalistic astrology permits us to go much farther. At this point, the "pure" scientists are shaking their heads in despair, but once again, the Zohar makes it clear: the human body is directly related to the universe as a whole and to every one of the stars, even those in the most remote galaxies, millions of light-years away.

As a result, an in-depth analysis of the human body will open new vistas of the heavens, and in turn, studying the heavens will allow us to penetrate the depths of the internal energy forces of the body. This places the Kabbalist in a position to understand the internal energy force and intelligence of the planets, revealing a new understanding of the laws of nature from the sub-atomic realm to the makeup of the universe.

If internal consciousness determines the ultimate physical manifestation, then by using astrology to learn the internal consciousness of a human being, one can confidently predict what that individual is likely to become in life. The end of any physical state is first determined by thought. The thought of a thief results in stealing, that of a violent person in mayhem or murder, that of one connected to the Tree of Life in philanthropy and personal success.

Consciousness is the universe and because knowledge is connection, as we think, so we will be—a point that should stand as a vital warning. Our thoughts are not idle. They can make us and they can break us, according to whether or not we are willing to control them, but if we do control them, there is no end to the miracles they can make manifest in our lives.

Words Are Weapons

Consciousness is forever. It never ages; it is eternal. As a result, thoughts conceived in a moment of haste go on forever. Yet, how often do we allow ourselves little indulgences of unbridled thought—momentary flashes of greed, lust, envy, and hatred. Thinking ourselves exempt from penalty, we can't imagine that the thoughts we create go on forever and cause immeasurable harm, time and time again.

Words mirror the thoughts that create them, and like the thoughts, they, too, are immortal. Some words are as lethal as bombs and bullets.

Let us say, for example, that in a momentary fit of temper a person verbally threatens bodily harm to someone who persists in annoying him or her. Later, of course, upon reflection, the person cools off and forgets the whole thing. No harm done, right? Wrong! Consciousness is not subject to entropy. The evil intent voiced in an irrational moment is a force of consciousness, and unless it is consciously removed by the one who voiced it, it remains forever. Unless the phrase, "God forbid," is attached to the threat, the person who has been threatened remains in grave danger because the negativity, unclaimed and left intact, devolves immediately to the Opponent. He seizes it and keeps it, in a manner of speaking, for a rainy day when the person at whom it has been directed, in a moment of human weakness, allows the Opponent to deliver it.

The worst thing a person can say to another human being is, "Goddamn you" (God forbid—don't even write it as an example without removing it), because that expresses an active desire that the Light of the Creator be forever cut off from the person so targeted—truly the worst fate imaginable. Of course, one who constantly curses other people eventually will fall victim to his or her own evil tongue, which is doing nothing more than expressing the life-devouring negativity held inside.

The Evil Eye

Unfortunately, a sin also can sink the innocent bystander who goes through life naively insisting that there is no such thing as a curse and consequently making no effort to erect a security shield against such a thing. The Kabbalist knows that the concept of a curse is far more than just a superstition born of ignorance. That is why Kabbalah has specific prayers designed to protect against the evil eye. Do not be too quick to shrug off such protections as talismans of a weird witchcraft. The evil eye is very real and very deadly and, as with all tenets and practices of Kabbalah, it has its grounding in the Bible.

The Book of Numbers tells the tale of Balaam, an early-day sorcerer of sorts who was called upon by the Moabites to curse the Israelites who were about to invade their land. He could have done it, too, because according to Rabbi Shimon bar Yohai,

Balaam carried with him "the eye of the destroying negative force" that is capable of consuming anyone or anything on which the "eye" falls (further discussed in my book The Power of One). In short, the evil eye is possessed by anyone who is a willing channel of the negative force of destruction, and there is no shortage of such persons in today's world. In the case of those early Israelites, Balaam gave up after seeing that the power of the Shechinah covered the Israelites and rendered them invulnerable to his evil talent.

Evidence of the Shechinah is seen on the person, the modern Kabbalist, in the form of a bit of red twine tied about the left wrist. This is twine that has been consecrated in Israel at the tomb of Rachel, who represents the material world of Malchut. It is knotted seven times to match the seven verses of the Ana beko'ach, which is recited as each knot is tied. Kabbalistic literature contends that the primary cause of cancer is the evil tongue by which the evil eye is activated, and that the eye is responsible for most, if not all, otherwise unexplained deaths.

Words are weapons; thoughts can kill. Use both with care.

Metaphysical Muggings

The evil eye and the enraged curse are not the only means by which the Opponent can trip us up. We do his work for him almost every day. How often do we do something destructive, then look back and chastise ourselves, saying, "How could I have made that kind of mistake? I'm not an idiot; how could I do such an idiotic thing?" The answer, of course, is that we simply have been careless. By some negative act or thought, we have left the door open for the Opponent who always is eager to enter our lives. Given an opening, he can afflict us even through our friends and loved ones.

There is a Kabbalistic parable that tells the tale of two brothers. They loved each other deeply and were equals, economically and socially. But the younger brother had something the elder brother lacked—children. The older brother deeply wanted children but he and his wife were unable to conceive them. As a result, he adored his nieces and nephews all the more fiercely because they were surrogates. Then, because the aching lack of children of his own still festered beneath his genuine love of family, it started happening. Every time the man visited his brother, the sight of the children activated that lack on a level almost too deep for self-detection until ultimately, after every visit with their beloved uncle, the children became ill. The longer he was around them, the sicker they became, succumbing to the negative waves of resentment emanating from his unresolved envy. The man did not seek negativity, nor did he consciously aim it at his nieces and nephews. But, unfortunately for the children, neither did he detect it in himself and consciously reject it.

Hauntings and Possessions

Because consciousness is the only reality, even apparently inanimate objects, like the mummy in the British museum, can absorb and hold it for long periods of time. Never for a moment think that Halloween comes only on October 31—or that it is a holiday for children. We are shielded by veils of mercy from the "ghoulies and ghosties" and a grim host of other things that really are out there. Without the veils, the Zohar says, we would take one look at the hellish host that surrounds us and die of fright.

Halloween is with us 24 hours a day, 365 days a year. To call its forces and minions mere superstition, or to write off evidence of their malice as unconnected coincidences, is to walk blindly into the metaphysical minefield the Opponent has prepared for the unwary.

One moves into a house only after the previous occupants have departed, but they leave their thought consciousness behind, and if that consciousness is steeped in negativity and malice, the new owner soon may discover that the place is "haunted." The haunting can range from vague feelings of depression and distress to the raucous violence of the poltergeist. If someone has died there under bad circumstances—usually someone constitutionally unable to accept the passage of death—what is left behind is called a ghost.

Such things, if they occur, can be purged with meditation and prayer. Demonic possession is another matter. Happily for the human race, possession is rare, but it does exist. The demons, by whatever names they may take, cannot seize a human soul unless the human in question actively, even if unconsciously, seeks them out. But demons are real, and once established, they completely displace the original soul with results even more horrific than those depicted in the Hollywood terror flick, The Exorcist. Charles Manson, Richard Speck, David Berkowitz, Jeffrey Dahmer—for these, the veils of mercy were torn, and instead of dying of fright they went mad at what they saw. To their peril, and the peril of their victims, they also became part of what they saw.

Fortunately for the rest of us, there is another sort of possession. It is that which takes place when a guardian angel invades our DNA and holds the metaphysical monstrosities of the Opponent at bay. Demons and angels alike are raw wavelengths of energy. They are highly intelligent, quite powerful, and, like other entities discussed here, very real, even if they do exist on the far frontiers of reality. Their missions are either to destroy or to preserve, and they pursue their aim with a single-minded dedication.

It is the demon that twists a human soul into what thereafter can only be called "a thing." It is the angel who locks the door against the demon and occasionally ties up traffic on the way to the airport so that his or her charge misses the plane that is destined to crash shortly after takeoff. Most people are as unaware of the angel as they are of the demon, so long as the demon inhabits somebody else. Only the Kabbalists clearly recognize them. Because they know themselves and face the universe with certainty, the Kabbalists control both of them.

CHAPTER 11

ANGELS

He shall give His angels charge over thee, to keep thee in all thy ways.

—*Psalm 91:11*

They're Everywhere

One Newtonian law of physics not overturned by the new science of quantum mechanics is this: every action has an equal, opposite reaction. To paraphrase that dictum: for every devil on the payroll of the Opponent, there is an angel that can be on yours, if you know how to get in touch with it. As a matter of fact, whether you know it or not, you already have a personal model, called a guardian angel, that you, alone, have designed and constructed.

We have explored the dark and dangerous corridors of the Opponent's metaphysical world, where unclean monstrosities lurk just beyond the veils of vision, and soul possession is a grim possibility for the unwary. Now we must investigate its opposite environment, one of wholesomeness and Light where some of the most brilliant and fascinating creatures in the Creator's universe dwell. They, too, can possess us, but their embrace is one of love, certainty, and security. Angel possession is a possession much to be desired.

For centuries, artists have portrayed angels as ethereal humanoid beings, soaring upon wings of iridescent Light. Like the Creator Himself, angels are constituted of pure, raw, sentient, metaphysical energy. They radiate that energy at various wavelengths, depending upon their individual missions. God created them in the endless world both as instruments of His will and to balance the cosmos. Given the level of an angel's consciousness, it easily might appear in human form should necessity mandate it, but angels essentially are without gender, wings, or any radiance beyond that given to them by the Light.

The Dark One

As manifestations of the Lord's beneficence, Angels represent good, not evil, though like the raw current in an electrical circuit, they are not judgmental and must be handled with knowledge, caution, and kavanah. As with all things in this dualistic physical universe, however, there is one angel whose mission it is to strike terror to the human heart by playing tricks with truth. He—and we will give him gender in this case—is known as the Angel of Death. He made his debut on the stage of humanity in the role of a serpent in that passion play involving the Garden of Eden, and his most famous line as he urged Eve to go ahead and taste the forbidden fruit of the Tree of Knowledge was, "You will not surely die."

That moment of mendacity instantly gave him two titles that he bears to this day: Angel of Death and Father of Lies. We simply call him the Opponent, and the death he represents as its dark angel is, like everything else in physical Malchut, an illusion. But the Opponent is very good at what he does, and as long as he can strike fear of death in the hearts of men and women, he can divert them from the quest for life, which really is what all of us are here to pursue. As soon as the Opponent is evicted once and for all by that collective surge in human consciousness that soon will open the door to the Messiah, the Angel of Death will become little more than an unremembered dream.

Power Lines

But a host of other God-created angels remain on the side of the Light and they are essential to the very fabric of our lives. The mightiest of them are Gabriel, Michael, Raphael, and Uriel— the four archangels whose fame is greater than any figures from mythology or imagination. Metaphorically, they anchor "the four corners of the Earth" and serve the Creator much as human cabinet secretaries serve the President of the United States. Like high profile holders of those cabinet posts, they get the best press and, consequently, are the best known. But there is a fundamental difference between the archangels and their human counterparts in the White House. Angels are "fixed" creatures, capable of doing only what they are programmed to do. We humans can be charitable and benign one minute and harsh and judgmental in the next. They cannot. They work only on their individual missions, and they act only when called upon.

The four famed archangels are represented on the Tree of Life, which is where they dwell, by the first four Sfirot below the upper triad. Michael is Chesed, the seed containing the potential manifestation of all things. But powerful as he is when roused, Michael can do nothing until he is called into being, either by the Light or by a human using the first verse of the Ana beko'ach to alert him that a specific mission is about to be proposed.

Across the way, at the midpoint of the left column, stands Gabriel as Gvurah. Gabriel is the facilitator designated to carry out the supplicant's mission as soon as its essence has been passed to him by Michael in Chesed. That essence passes to Gabriel through the Sfira of Tiferet where Uriel holds sway. Tiferet, and consequently Uriel, represents the restriction necessary to activate the circuitry of the Tree of Life. He is, in effect, the filament of the light bulb that glows as soon as the "hot wire" of negative Gvurah meets the "neutral," or positive pole, of Chesed.

Finally, in Malchut, Raphael represents all the manifestations of the other three. It is here that the potential triggered through contact with Michael and handed off to Gabriel and Uriel finally becomes manifest. The four archangels are the most powerful in the heavenly hierarchy, but they are no more important than their more humbly placed colleagues. Angels of lower rank actually do shift-work as the contingent in charge of a given day is replaced by the one responsible for the day that follows. Each has a different purpose, but for all, the central mission is to block and frustrate the Opponent and all his works. Not to believe in, and hence never call upon, angels can be truly perilous, since that leaves the Opponent in charge.

Angels are powers less akin to human society than to nature. Recently, near the heart of the enormous hydroelectric power grid centered in the Pacific Northwest, wind-lashed tree branches fell across four little power lines, shorting them out. Normally, one would not consider four individual lines of major consequence, but when they were broken, nine states went dark in the domino effect that followed.

Angels constitute a metaphysical power grid, channeling the Light of the Creator into our physical universe. The archangels may carry a load measurable in gigawatts, but knock out one or two of their "lesser" components—perhaps those angels who, when directed by kavanah, carry messages of prayer to the Lord—and we have a blackout in Malchut.

It Is Up to Us

Of all the ranks and hierarchies of what most frequently is called the Heavenly Host, none captures the interest and imagination of the ordinary human more than the one called guardian angel. Even the devout atheist may be heard to comment in the aftermath of a terrifying close encounter with catastrophe, "My guardian angel must have been looking out for me." In fact, failure to accept the power of such a guardian generally reveals nothing more than an ego problem—the inability to come to grips with the idea that there is more to reality than what the five senses perceive.

Recognition that unseen metaphysical forces really do exist necessarily leads to the disturbing suspicion that one is not in total control of life after all. And without the guardian angel, or the practice of Kabbalah, that is terribly true.

Unlike other angelic forces, the guardian is not a gift from God. The guardian angel is your own construct—a creation on which you have worked over many incarnations. As you bring the tikkune, or baggage, from your most immediate past life into this one, you also bring your guardian angel, who is nothing more or less than what you have made him or her.

We are, after all, co-creators with God, a bit of whom lives inside each of us, along with a bit of the Holy Temple, a bit of the Ark of the Covenant, and a bit of every sacred thing that the Creator has given us. Thus, over the course of many incarnations, we create our guardian angels with the words we say, the thoughts we entertain, the deeds we do, and according to the Zohar, the intensity of our interest in spiritual things.

The Blueprint

The most vital ingredient in constructing a guardian angel, the Zohar specifically says, is study of and familiarity with the Torah. Because of the efficacy of Hebrew letters, the Torah is necessarily the most efficient tool in this exercise. But as we have emphasized, Kabbalah is not a religion. Like all valid metaphysical systems, Kabbalah draws its power from the source of Him who sits in the focus of all religion, and all texts thus derived are vehicles of that power. All can be used to create a guardian angel if the seeker is willing to study them in depth.

If the job of creating a guardian angel is properly done, the angel in question will be wise, truthful, powerful, and able to see into the future in order to protect its master. In virtually every plane crash, someone can be found who was tied up in traffic, who took a cab that broke down on its way to the airport, or who made a wrong turn, got lost, and missed the fatal flight. In nearly every case, that delay was the result of a powerful guardian angel and the lesson it offers is this: never become frustrated and enraged at delays and roadblocks. It is true that they sometimes are the work of the Opponent; most of the time, they are the work of your guardian who only wants to shield you from impending disaster.

But angel-making is a lot like playing the stock market. The angel's relative merits, or the lack of them, rise and fall as the individual's soul growth rises and falls. If you enhance your soul, you enhance your angel; if you diminish your soul, your angel is diminished. The truly evil actually produce guardians who, in their degeneracy, simply give up and go to work for the Opponent. You don't want to know where they lead their creators.

What You Give Is What You Get

The Zohar notes that some guardian angels are totally honest, emerging directly from the study of holy texts or fulfillment of those textual requirements. Others are partially truthful, and still others, while not evil, are more prone to falsehood. All emerge from levels of consciousness in which the mind and intentions of the angel-maker customarily dwell. The most powerful guardians wind up in the company of prophets, biblical or secular, who know with certainty what the future will bring. But those born of or subsequently diminished by desire to receive for the self alone with all its attendant negativity are little more than ignorant stooges who, far from guiding and protecting their charges, consistently lead them astray.

People who, through religion or cultural custom, have come to regard the Lord as an anthropomorphic father figure, may find all of this disturbing. In their eyes, like a good earthly father, He is in constant attendance of His children, alternately rewarding them for good behavior and punishing them when they are naughty. They thank Him profusely when times are good, and when catastrophe strikes, they lower their eyes and accept the pain as His inscrutable will. "The Lord works in mysterious ways," the Jew may whisper. "Inshallah," the Muslim may say with a shrug. "Thy will be done," the Christian may sigh. But the truth lies elsewhere.

We and we alone are the masters of our own destinies. We choose every minute of the day whether we will receive for the self alone or receive for the sake of sharing, and with every word, thought, or action, we modify the guardian angel we have created. We bring upon ourselves the heel of oppression, pain, and suffering, or we open the door to receive the full beneficence of the Creator—a beneficence that pours forth like sunlight, aimed at no individual but available to all who will avail themselves of it. The Creator of the universe does not busy Himself with the little details of our individual lives; He leaves that up to us.

The Kabbalist must understand that, in order to manifest certainty, he or she must be capable of a childlike trust in the Light of the Creator. At the same time, he or she must avoid the desire to receive for the self alone, the urge that makes us childish. Kabbalah is for grownups. If we want a guardian angel with a badge, a crystal ball, and a metaphysical PhD, we have to work for it.

Fortunately, with the spread of Kabbalah and its ability to elevate human consciousness, angel quality gets better every day. Now, an end to the Opponent's reign of violence and chaos is on the immediate horizon. Every one of us is the instrument by which a quantum reality of Messiah will become a reality.

Each one of us is God.

CHAPTER 12

FINALLY FREE

"So let freedom ring!"

—*Rev. Dr. Martin Luther King Jr.*

The New Millennia

For centuries, the wisdom of Kabbalah has been suppressed, both by those who fear it because they do not know what it is, and by those who do know what it is and don't want it taught to the world at large because they fear it would be harmful to the uninitiated.

But in this new millennium, the Tree of Life reality is emerging as inexorably as lilacs in springtime, and as it does, some Jewish and non-Jewish religious leaders are likely to fear it as a competing doctrine that threatens to steal away their congregations. In the Jewish community, where the few who have taught Kabbalah have been constrained by tradition from giving it to anyone but a male over the age of 40, many view its spread to non-Jews and to men and women of all ages as a betrayal of the doctrines of Judaism.

Both sides will be wrong.

Lest this argument be turned into a rallying cry for further suppression of the truth, it should be stated that the author of this book is in no way pushing for the total integration of religious beliefs or proselytizing for a unified religion. Indeed, it never was the intention of the Creator to consider the Bible an instrument for religion; rather, the Bible is the code of our universe and Kabbalah is its deciphering instrument. And, though its tenets recognize the truth of a Supreme Being, Kabbalah itself is no more a religion than is quantum physics, which so remarkably resembles it.

Kabbalah presents a system by which the universal features of humankind can be unified; it does not affect the individual factors that make up human diversity. Religious multiplicity exists to permit adherents to advance their own responsibilities and knowledge. Yet, there is a higher authority that maintains the final say in all of our activities. Many may reject this notion of authority; nonetheless, there are universal laws and principles that we can neither resist nor hope to change.

The Zohar tells us the intent of the Creator when He summoned Moses was to use the giving of the law to the Israelites as a means of returning the cosmos to the state in which it existed prior to the sin of Adam. In short, through the metaphysical process described earlier, He sought to reverse the sin, even as water was drawn from the rock, by rolling the event back into its undifferentiated, potential state, then cloning a new DNA sequence to reestablish paradise on earth. Humans then would live forever, free of the pain and suffering that now marks our brief passage here. The effort was doomed to fail even as the two evil magicians were destined to accompany the Israelites in their trek out of Egypt. By creating the golden calf, they replaced the beautiful sequences of immortality with their own corrupted sequences of death, short-circuiting the Lord's intent. In so doing, they concealed the Light of the Creator from the people and rendered the intent of the Decalogue inoperable.

But how, one might ask, can the all-powerful, all-knowing Creator of the universe be foiled by mere human agencies? The reason, of course, is that He gave us free will. When we rejected His beneficence, he restricted it and imprisoned the Light so that we alone, by our own restriction of the desire to receive, could free it. Thus Adam had the freedom to sin in the garden of Eden; the wicked Erev Rav of Sinai had the freedom to interfere in the process of re-creation; and today, each and every one of us has the freedom to work evil to the detriment of good.

Death to Death

A new re-creation will occur, and when it does, it again will employ the Hebrew letters contained in the Decalogue. The letters of the Ten Commandments constitute the precise formulation of a DNA sequence that can bring death to the idea of death itself. Death, the ultimate fear, can be eradicated, along with chaos and all the derivatives of chaos that adhere to it. Spiritual Light, when channeled through proper creative sequences, is capable of removing every vestige of the illusory feature of the physical reality of evil, which is based on a desire to receive for the self alone, thus permitting the dominion of good, or desire to receive for the sake of sharing.

This was the phenomenon of the revelation on Mount Sinai. It was not an isolated event; every generation must return to the revelation of the Tree of Life reality if we are to secure any vestige of sanity and order in our lives. The biblical events and so-called Jewish holidays give us the precise indication of when we can tap into the awesome cosmic power of the Tree of Life universe. But more important, the revelation provides the coded instructions of those holidays, which actually serve as nothing more than vital microchips in the Tree of Life circuitry, to designate the channels by which we embark upon and travel through the cosmic journey. Once the cosmic connection has been bonded in unity with the Tree of Life, we have crossed the threshold where past, present, and future combine. Revelation then becomes an ever-present event freeing spiritual Light.

Because their level of spirituality was incompatible with the power of the DNA sequence offered to them by the revelation, the Israelites could not harness it and they eventually perished in the wilderness. The ugly Erev Rav Jew—the faction that pulled the Israelites down in the desert—is responsible for a world subsequently torn daily by violence and chaos. Their lack of tolerance and compassion is what has maintained the never-ending nightmare that has been the hallmark of 2,000 years of Jewish misery and, by extension, the misery of most of the world.

But now, in this absolutely unique and unprecedented moment in history, the revelation takes on a new significance that was not readily accessible to earlier generations. Religion, once the glory of civilization, has failed dismally to keep pace with the changing times. The state of the world has literally coerced us into rethinking our priorities and actions and, at this stage of its evolution, we stand not on the edge of disaster but on the threshold of a quantum leap into the unimaginable.

The Second Revelation

The Zohar states that "all the celestial treasures and hidden mysteries which were not revealed to succeeding generations will be revealed." This will accomplish what the Erev Rav managed to block so many millennia ago in the Sinai desert; it will re-create the original revelation.

This is what this book is all about. Rabbi Shimon bar Yohai confirmed that the messianic era will bring with it revelation and a richness representing the infusion of the Light of the Creator through all the worlds. The dawn of a new world will appear, and along with it, spiritual energy will begin to liberate men and women from their ignorance, bringing them spiritual awakening and lives of well-being.

The first verse of the Ana beko'ach is an example of the phenomenal changes that are weaving themselves through the consciousness of humankind. Kabbalistic tools, once hidden, now are revealed to the layperson. Concepts such as control over our destiny, removal of serious medical impairments, restoration of limbs and organs, and even public discussions of immortality are being aired.

The past 2,000 years of chaos have left an indelible mark upon the consciousness of the human race. The vast majority of traditional scientists, clergy, and laypeople have not been able to entertain the idea that the human mind can influence physical reality. Yet the scriptures ask us to accept, without question, the proposition that consciousness can indeed transcend the laws of physics. The human mind possesses a force sufficient to influence and even alter material essence. The Kabbalah tells us that we rule both the terrestrial and the celestial realms.

The needless battlefields and the world's uncounted cemeteries attest to the replacement of this glorious concept and to the consequent corruption of our existence. But today, the opportunity to permanently end human suffering through the agency of the sequences of the Light of the Creator never has been greater. It is the dawn of a genuinely new era, a time in which all evil is abolished, all good is manifest, and all things are possible. And make no mistake; it will be here sooner than you know.

Kabbalist Rav Berg was born in Williamsburg, New York, into a family with a long rabbinical tradition. After studying at Beit Midrash Gavoha in Lakewood, New Jersey, Rav Berg was ordained at the renowned rabbinical seminary, Torah VaDaat, in Williamsburg.

In the spring of 1964, Rav Berg met his master, Rav Yehuda Brandwein, author of The Steps of the Ladder, the commentary to the Tikune Ha Zohar, and unquestionably the greatest Kabbalist of his time. Rav Brandwein provided the wisdom and guidance that enabled Rav Berg to make the transition from student to the most influential Kabbalist of this generation. And while it was with awe and wonder that Rav Berg agreed to carry the torch, it soon became his life's mission to make the study of Kabbalah available to everyone.

Rav Berg and his wife, Karen, have been pioneers in declaring Kabbalah a source of spiritual knowledge for all humankind. They transformed The Kabbalah Centre from an exclusive place of study to an open forum of learning, for anyone interested in achieving self-improvement through spiritual realization.

For the past three decades, Rav Berg has dedicated himself to continuing the legacy passed on to him by his teacher. His principal contributions to spreading the word of Kabbalah include the development of the curriculum of all The Kabbalah Centre programs, as well as the authorship and publication of over a dozen books, including Immortality; Wheels of the Soul; The Power of One; Miracles, Mysteries and Prayers; and many more. Such prodigious scholarship has made him the most prolific Kabbalistic scholar of this generation.

As well as co-directing The Centre, teaching, and updating The Centre's curriculum, Rav Berg still finds time to lecture around the world on the spiritual laws of Kabbalah and the meaning of life. Renowned and respected wherever he goes, he often meets privately with world leaders to help encourage peace, particularly in volatile regions. He also acts as an advisor to other spiritual and religious leaders of all faiths. Rav Berg is truly the Kabbalist for our times.

Kabbalah Publishing Reading Group Guide

Introduction	• Have you ever thought of spirituality as a technology before you read *Taming Chaos*? • Do you think it's possible for humans to control their destiny? • Is it possible to live in a reality free from all forms of chaos? What do you imagine that would look like?
Chapter One: **The Tree of Life and The Tree of Knowledge**	• Why is it important to create change on the seed level? • What is the desire to receive for the self alone? Where does it appear in your life? • What are some of the benefits of being proactive? • What is Bread of Shame? How do you see this concept at work in your life?
Chapter Two: **Adversaries and Allies**	• What is the opponent's job? How does he help us? • Why is it difficult for us to see simple concepts as powerful? Why must powerful wisdom be simple?
Chapter Three: **Spiritual Tools**	• What steps must we take to gain control of our lives? • How are prayer and meditation related? What is the purpose of kavanah? How does kavanah relate to prayer? • After trying the meditation, reflect on your experience. What was it like? • Have you ever been to any of the energy centers listed? What was the energy like? What is the importance of Jerusalem? What is the function of the temple? • What experiences have you had using the 72 Names?
Chapter Four: **Channels of Energy**	• What does it mean to "bless the Lord"? How does reciting a blessing help us?
Chapter Five: **Ana Beko'ach**	• Take a moment and do the Ana Beko'ach. How do you feel after completing it? • Do the prayer daily for a few days. What experiences have you had after doing the Ana Beko'ach? • Has the introduction of the Ana Beko'ach into your life changed the way you act or see things?
Chapter Six: **Science and Spirit**	• What are the three types of light? What do they do? • What is meant by 'as above, so below'?
Chapter Seven: **Sickness and Health**	• What is the idea behind allopathic or conventional Western medicine? How does this differ from Kabbalistic ideas? • How do the Sfirot help us heal? • What happens when we turn on the Light? • What happens when we feel stressed? • What can we do spiritually to stay healthy?
Chapter Eight: **Beyond the End**	• Why do we experience pain and suffering? • Do you think immortality is achievable?
Chapter Nine: **Consciousness and Creation**	• What is the power of consciousness? • What do you think about mind over matter?
Chapter Ten: **Dangerous Intentions**	• How is Kabbalistic astrology different from conventional astrology? • What is the power of speech? • What is evil eye and how can we protect ourselves from it?
Chapter Eleven: **Angels**	• What are angels? What is their job? • How can we use the four archangels to assist us in our lives? • What is a guardian angel? How do our actions affect it? What is a demon?
Chapter Twelve: **Finally Free**	• How can we create lasting fulfillment in our lives?

If you have any questions about the book or your experiences, please contact us at 1.800.KABBALAH and talk to one of our student support representatives.